Green Mount Culinary

A Culinary Tour of Green Mount Cemetery

❧Contents❧

During the early years of writing Old Line Plate, I sometimes imagined a cemetery picnic at the grave of Frederick Philip Stieff, who compiled a great collection of Maryland's recipes, "Eat, Drink & Be Merry in Maryland," in 1932. As I wrote about more and more people and recipes, the Green Mount burials began to add up. I started envisioning a whole tour. After all, death and food have a peculiar link in our cultures, from graveside offerings to the droves of food that caring friends and family will send in a time of mourning, to the food served at funerals themselves.

After some losses of my own, my feelings about the project shifted. Quirky history is still a part of it, but I have gained more of a sense of responsibility for and communion with the dead and their memories. I've found a catharsis in spending time among them.

When I walk the grounds of Green Mount Cemetery, I see echoes from my research into the ever-changing story of Maryland food. So much is here: enslavers and Confederates who co-opted Black cooking into a regional identity; reformists and suffragettes who used food to further a cause; politicians who laid the foundation of Baltimore's reality over tables decked with terrapin and canvas-back duck; entrepreneurs who built up the city's industrial power; every-day people who went humbly about their lives and meals. Imperfect lives that paint a complicated picture of what is and was Baltimore's cuisine.

The stories they left behind are recipes. The rest is for me to piece together. A recipe is a tangible gift passed from the dead to the living; a gustatory seance at the memorial table, drawn from the past and brought here into a fleeting present. When visitors circulate the cemetery walkways, we are doing nothing new in the history of Green Mount. Just seven years after the cemetery's founding, in 1845, Green Mount's treasurer assured lot-holders that visits on Sundays would be restricted to themselves and their families, to limit crowds of "gay and thoughtless persons" who assembled there. In 1848, the annual report considered the issue "of recreation and public amusement under the system of almost free admission." At the time, the idea of preserving nature was foreign to most Americans. Parks were rare. Baltimore's Druid Hill Park first opened in 1860, and Patterson Park was a smaller public walkway until it was expanded that same year.

Green Mount was the fourth "rural cemetery" established in the U.S., fairly early on a trend that was sweeping the nation. As downtown church burial grounds grew increasingly over-crowded, they became places of fester and disease, polluting the local water-supply. They were prone to grave-robbery and vandalism.

When Boston's Mount Auburn was founded in 1831, cramped graveyards gave way to sprawling 'cemeteries', built like pleasure gardens and arboretums. The July 1839 dedication of Green Mount featured ceremonies including an opening prayer, a Hymn composed for the occasion, an oration, and a performance of the Musical Association of Baltimore singing a chorale of Oratorio of St. Paul by Felix Mendelssohn. An "efficient police" was in attendance "to see that the regulations of the occasion are observed." Right from the start, the garden cemetery was walking a fine line between a place of mourning and a place of pleasure. It is a concern to this day, and cemetery regulations remind visitors to be mindful of ongoing mourning and burial services.

I imagine the different Baltimores inhabited by my "Green Mount people." A city that invented bottle caps and the Ouija Board, from where so much of the nation's food was packed and shipped. A town where former enslavers and people who fought to preserve slavery walked the streets, sold goods, entered politics, and shared recipes with impunity.

When Green Mount was founded, the cemetery was more segregated than the city itself. In 1874, Martha Ann Atavis, a woman enslaved by Dr. John Whitridge, was buried in Green Mount with the family who enslaved her. This exception to the rule underscores the ugly truth of many of my recipes. The Thomas family recipe books contain dozens of recipes whose true origins will never be fully uncovered. We do know that a relative of Whitridge, John Hanson Thomas, enslaved a cook named Sibby Grant, whose recipe for Stewed Kidneys is attributed in the cookbook of Alice Whitridge Thomas.

Many of the true architects of Baltimore cuisine are buried in Mount Auburn, the cemetery of the Sharp Street Methodist Church. Early caterers like J. Logan Jenkins, and those like Henry Cummings, who successfully followed in their footsteps, are buried there. Their businesses helped build Baltimore into "the gastronomic metropolis of the Union," a reputation that persisted into the Civil Rights Era.

The rub is that caterers rarely left behind recipes. Written recipes can't capture skill and talent. In this way, Green Mount is like cookbooks themselves, containing a mere façade of a meal; a version of history, the story as written by the oppressors.

That has never stopped me from digging deeper to take a closer look. I still believe that under the glare of history, the past can be exhumed, the story retold, and the recipe rewritten.

3

Maryland Fried Chicken

Mrs. Benjamin Chew Howard
1801-1890
Section A, plot 5

As a dish that had been prepared by enslaved people, and later by professional Black caterers, Maryland Fried Chicken is a fitting symbol of the complicated culture of dining in Baltimore from the time after the Civil War up through the 1940s.

The rise and fall of Maryland's culinary prestige alongside Jim Crow through the Civil Rights era may not be purely coincidence. The dishes and settings were tied up in a culture that revered yet pigeonholed and belittled the Black people who created, prepared and served Maryland's signature dishes.

One of the early written recipes for Maryland Fried Chicken appeared in a popular 1873 cookbook "Fifty Years in A Maryland Kitchen," by Mrs. Benjamin Chew Howard, nee Jane Gilmore.

Jane Grant Gilmor was born in 1801 to merchant and art collector William Gilmor and his Virginian wife, Mary Ann Drysdale Gilmor. In 1818, she became the wife of Benjamin Chew Howard, a politician and businessman. She moved to Belvidere, the Howards' estate in what is now the Mt. Vernon neighborhood of Baltimore, near where the Belvedere hotel was later built.

Over the course of Jane's life, the world changed dramatically. She spent most of her time as a plantation mistress at Belvidere, overseeing the kitchen and an enslaved staff whose names we may never know. The manor became known for hospitality.

In 1842, the Howards sold Belvidere. Jane wrote a letter to her husband, brokenhearted at moving, and lamenting how life was changing. The letter mentions that Jane hoped "Caroline [would] be again in the kitchen."

Jane Howard's vantage point must have changed as Baltimore grew and densified around her, and the country transformed even more. In 1837, Benjamin Chew Howard wrote of "abolition which that miserable state of Vermont is meddling with." In 1861 he ran for the governorship of Maryland under a "states rights" platform. He lost.

Mrs. Howard dedicated herself to "Southern Relief" after the war - raising funds for formerly wealthy families whose fortunes had turned downward.

When Benjamin died in 1872, one obituary in the Charleston South Carolina Daily Courier wrote "When friends were rare, and gaunt want came pinching, Benjamin Chew Howard, and the revered ladies of his household, noiselessly as the dews of morning, but effectively as the meridian sun, lifted up many a bowed spirit." "The eye of many a Confederate window moistens with genuine sorrow," to learn of his death, the paper concluded.

"Fifty Years in a Maryland Kitchen" saw publication the year following Benjamin's death. With its lavish ingredients and massive quantities, Howard's book bore a subtle message of a fabled time of plenty and a life of ease — a Southern fantasy that continued to sell well into the civil rights era.

Howard's cookbook spoke to readers who upheld this fantasy, but also to plenty of people who just liked good food. For decades after its publication, newspapers continued to share Howard's recipes, often affixing the word "Maryland" to them, such as "Maryland Cream Waffles." Howard's recipe entitled "Fried Chickens" instructed readers to fry a brined chicken in lard and serve with a cream gravy seasoned with salt, pepper, and parsley.

The cream gravy, along with the traditional slow pan-frying, tends to demarcate Maryland Fried Chicken when it makes a rare appearance on modern menus, but the nature of the dish has been disputed from its inception. There isn't even agreement on what to call it: sometimes the dish bears the Frenchified moniker "Chicken a la Maryland," sometimes "Fried Chicken, Maryland Style." Occasionally its simply "Chicken Maryland."

In his 1951 historical profile of Baltimore, "The Amiable Baltimoreans," F. F. Beirne admitted that "in spite of all the enthusiastic praise of chicken á la Maryland, the scandal is that few persons even in Baltimore actually know what it is."

When Maryland Fried Chicken is mentioned today, the conversation is often spurred by a resurfacing of a menu from the Titanic. On April 14th, 1912, "Chicken A La Maryland" was served for luncheon in First Class.

Jane Howard died in 1890, and is buried in Green Mount with generations of her parents' family. She left five children; she was preceded in death by five others. Her name continued to be associated with Maryland cuisine, which enjoyed prestige for over a half-century after her death.

The recipes she left behind reflect the complicated and ugly histories of the ways imperialism and slavery benefited Maryland. They also contain traces of the obscured talent of anonymous cooks like Caroline.

While the legend of Belvidere hospitality has largely been forgotten, Howard's recipes still serve as references for all the Maryland classic dishes, from Maryland Fried Chicken to Deviled Crabs. Even her "Kitchen Pepper" recipe reveals a template for the seasoning that would become Old Bay.

Special Attention of Physicians is Respectfully Invited to the Remarks below, and to

Permit No.

Birth Place, { State or country, and how long in the United States, if of foreign birth.

Baltimore, Md

Duration of Residence in the City of Baltimore, *Life*

Place of Death, { Give Street and Number. } 918 N. Charles St

Cause of Death, { First (Primary), old age; no special organic

Second (Immediate), Heart failure

Duration of Last Sickness, 2 weeks

All the above information should be furnished by the Physician.

Place of Burial. Greenmount

Date of Burial, Nov 29th 1890

Undertaker, Welsh Entkins & Sons

Place of Business, Park & Saratoga

A la Chen
Medical

Address, 215 W. La

Extract from Regulations of the Board of Health to secure a full and correct record of in the City of Baltimore.

SECTION 2 And be it further enacted and ordained, That whenever any person shall die in the said city, the Physician who attended during his or her last sickness, or the Coroner, when the case comes under his no twenty-four hours after the death, to the Undertaker or other persons superintending the Burial, a certificate the same can be ascertained, the full name, sex, age and condition (whether married or single) of the person and date of death.

6

FRIED CHICKENS

Cut them up, and lay them in salt and water for several hours, then take them out and wipe them dry, season with pepper and salt, and then cover them with as much flour as they will hold. Have the lard boiling hot in a frying-pan, spider, or dutch oven, put in and fry the chickens very slowly, over hot coals (but not over the fire), turning and stirring them about to keep them from burning. It takes half an hour to fry them. Lay the chickens in a dish, pour off all the fat from the spider, put in a good-sized spoonful of butter, to which add cream, parsley, salt, and pepper; when hot, pour this over the chickens, and serve.

recipe from "Fifty Years in a Maryland Kitchen," Mrs. B.C. Howard, 1873

ears
in a
Maryland
Kitchen
Mrs B C Howard

R.M.S. "TITANIC"

APRIL 14, 1912.

LUNCHEON.

CONSOMMÉ FERMIER   COCKIE LEEKIE

FILLETS OF BRILL

EGG À L'ARGENTEUIL

CHICKEN À LA MARYLAND

CORNED BEEF, VEGETABLES, DUMPLINGS

FROM THE GRILL.

GRILLED MUTTON CHOPS

MASHED, FRIED & BAKED JACKET POTATOES

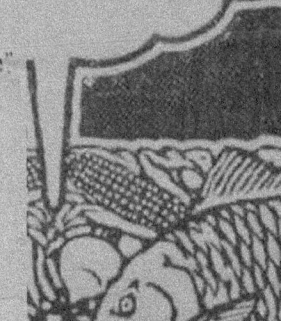

ꙮ Shad Roe a la Stieff ꙮ

Frederick Philip Stieff
1891-1964
Entrance Area, plot 61

"CREOLE DINNER: Waldo cooked the crawfish bisque in New Orleans and flew it to Baltimore by plane, and was the house guest of Fred Stieff. The most spectacular dish was the Cherry Jubilee, black heart cherries on Vanilla ice cream bathed in flaming cognac. The most distinguished guest was Mr. Henry Menkin. At the end of the meal Fred had to make a speech which was terrible and right in the middle of the speech Mr. Menkin just got up and walked out." — Baltimore Food & Wine Society notes, 1948

Frederick Philip Stieff is a character who has loomed larger than life for me since my blog's inception. I've fantasized about writing a screenplay about him, as I imagine him: traveling around the state collecting recipes.

Gregarious. Fanciful and prone to over-romanticizing the past and ideas about aristocracy. Jolly and ignorant. Asinine and racist.

I sometimes wonder what a masterpiece "Eat, Drink & Be Merry in Maryland" would be if Stieff were a more inquisitive person, if he had had productive conversations with friends of his like Gerald W. Johnson, who decried racism while defending segregation, and whose artichoke and eggplant recipes appear in "Eat, Drink & Be Merry."

If Stieff's work as a folklorist had been approached through a lens of equality, we might have had accounts and recipes of the Black chefs and home cooks who facilitated so much eating and drinking and merriment in Maryland.

Instead, Stieff continued the status quo, elevating the antebellum aristocratic fantasy underpinning the state's food culture. He may have managed to do even worse than cookbook authors before him. Stieff peppered his book with racist caricatures that belittled people who were major players in the food he loved so much.

Despite its deeply disappointing flaws, "Eat, Drink & Be Merry in Maryland" is a book I can't imagine my blog without.

Stieff was heir to the Stieff Piano business. The story goes that no one was buying pianos during the Great Depression and that left Fred with

8

plenty of time to pursue his culinary interests.

One imagines he would have found a way to do so even if there was more demand for "the poor man's Steinway" uprights that Frederick's father began manufacturing after emigrating from Germany. "Eat, Drink & Be Merry" captured recipes from all around the state, "Maryland cuisine" usually meant Eastern Shore dishes served in Baltimore dining rooms

And yet Stieff included bear steaks and venison from Western Maryland. Most notably, he included ample documentation of Maryland Stuffed Ham, which was not widely considered standard Maryland menu fare. Thanks to Stieff's collection, we have three versions of recipes for the St. Mary's County specialty - including one oddly from Frederick County.

For all his epicureanism, the only recipe associated with Stieff in his own book is for a fairly run of the mill spaghetti as made by his wife. But he had built himself up as such an authority on Maryland

FREDERICK PHILIP STIEFF
World citizen dies

food that he was called upon to contribute to other books such as the 1940 "America Cooks: Favorite Recipes from 48 States," by Cora, Rose, and Bob Brown. In his 1949 book "Dining with My Friends: Adventures with Epicures," Crosby Gaige included a number of Stieff's collected recipes, including a few of Stieff's own.

I mostly know of Gaige because some sources incorrectly assert that one of his cookbooks contained the first printed crab cake recipe, but according to the website Cocktail Kingdom "Crosby Gaige was a high profile theater producer, writer, epicure, gourmand, bon vivant and ubiquitous socialite—a difficult to avoid figure within the mid-Century New York mediasphere."

Frederick Stieff's recipe for "Shad Roe A La Stieff" is one of the more complicated shad roe recipes I've seen. He mixed the roe with cream sauce and served it in ramekins with Parmesan. The most common preparation is to simply fry the roe with some bacon and onions.

I can see the appeal of presenting the roe somewhat reformulated and

9

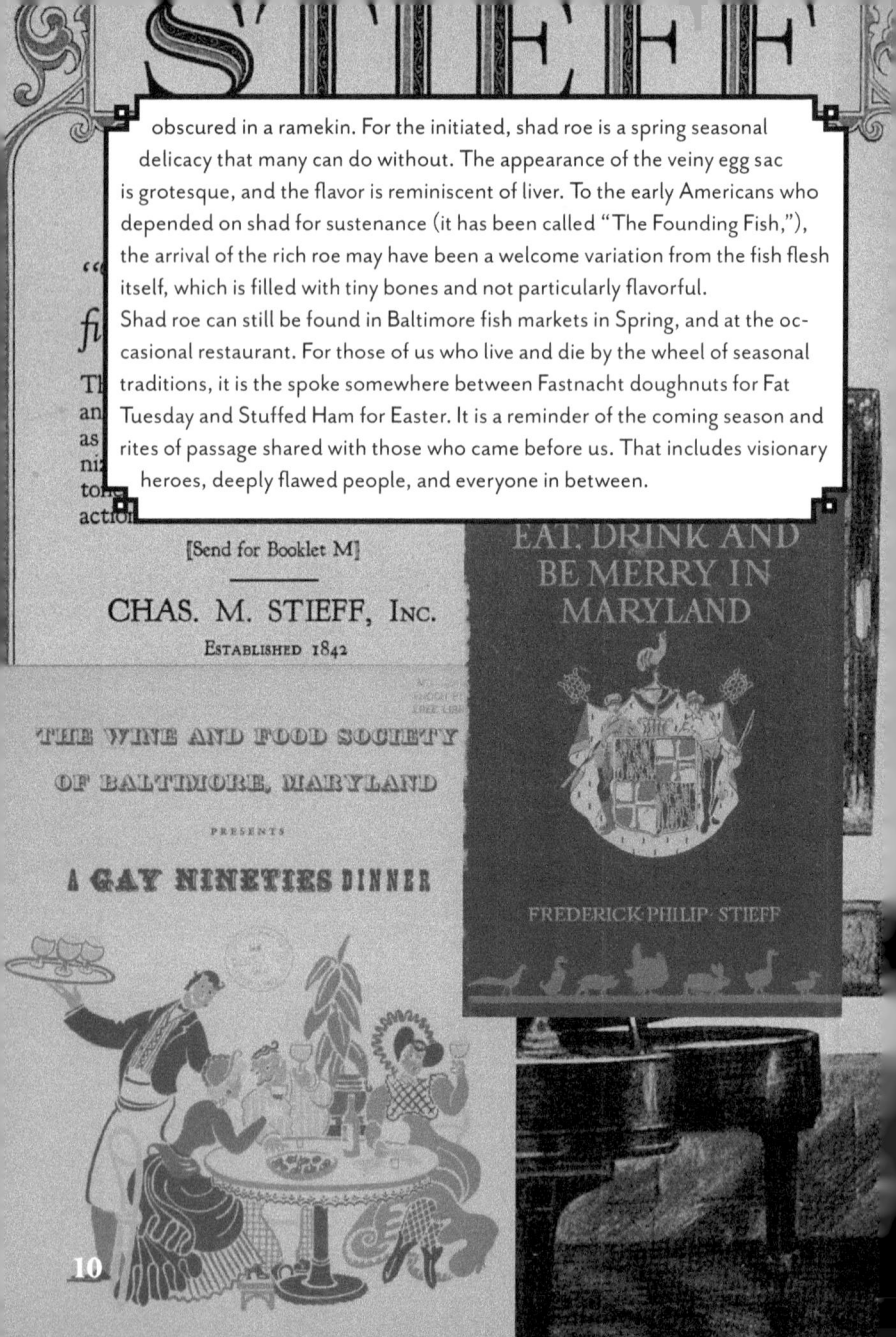

obscured in a ramekin. For the initiated, shad roe is a spring seasonal delicacy that many can do without. The appearance of the veiny egg sac is grotesque, and the flavor is reminiscent of liver. To the early Americans who depended on shad for sustenance (it has been called "The Founding Fish,"), the arrival of the rich roe may have been a welcome variation from the fish flesh itself, which is filled with tiny bones and not particularly flavorful.

Shad roe can still be found in Baltimore fish markets in Spring, and at the occasional restaurant. For those of us who live and die by the wheel of seasonal traditions, it is the spoke somewhere between Fastnacht doughnuts for Fat Tuesday and Stuffed Ham for Easter. It is a reminder of the coming season and rites of passage shared with those who came before us. That includes visionary heroes, deeply flawed people, and everyone in between.

[Send for Booklet M]

CHAS. M. STIEFF, Inc.

ESTABLISHED 1842

EAT, DRINK AND
BE MERRY IN
MARYLAND

THE WINE AND FOOD SOCIETY
OF BALTIMORE, MARYLAND

PRESENTS

A GAY NINETIES DINNER

FREDERICK PHILIP STIEFF

⟨ SHAD ROE A LA STIEFF ⟩

Parboil your shad roe 20 minutes. You will know the amount of shad roe to prepare dependent upon the number of your guests, their preferences, and capacities. The subsequent sauce should be prepared in due proportions.

Rub well your cockle-shells or ramekin dishes with garlic and grease well with butter. Skin roe and remove all veins, macerate roe to a consistency of caviar, mixing in a suitable proportion of garlic.

Prepare for a wastage of five per cent of your shad roe, due to skinning and veining.

Mix sauce of white wine, cream, pulverized sweet marjoram and rosemary, pepper, salt, paprika and well chopped parsley.

Pour sauce into shad roe and mix well. Fill shells or ramekin dishes with roe. Pour melted butter over each. Don't pack down. Sprinkle each with powdered Melba toast with very slight dusting of Parmesan, or Parmesan-type cheese. Run into oven to remain until surface is a golden brown. Before serving garnish with chopped parsley.

recipe from "Dining with My Friends: Adventures with Epicures," Crosby Gaige, 1949

⸎Celeried Oysters⸎

Ferdinand Claiborne Latrobe
1889-1944
Section EE, plot 22

Long before crab was king in Maryland, it was oysters that reigned the seafood industry. The presence of 3200 year old oyster middens persist as a testament to the sustaining power of the oyster, their shells deposited among shards of clay pots and bone tools by people who lived along the bay long before Europeans crossed the Atlantic. When John Smith explored in 1608, he found oysters lying "as thick as stones."

By the 1880s, the Chesapeake Bay supplied almost half of the oysters consumed in the western world. After the Civil War rattled and transformed the nation, the industry became fierce and bloody. In 1865, the Maryland General Assembly moved to regulate oyster harvesting, requiring permits and issuing them to state residents only. The profit was too great to resist, and water-men from Virginia and New England continued to dredge higher and higher into the bay. They came heavily armed and ready to exchange gunfire with the Maryland Oyster Police Force.

On dry land, diners in Baltimore, Philadelphia, New York and beyond continued to feed the demand for oysters. Unlike the meat of the Diamondback Terrapin, which had become an elite status signifier, oysters were available across the class strata of society. Hotels became famous for their oyster selections and preparations.

The "Oyster Wars" were still raging when Ferdinand Latrobe, Jr. published his 1940 book "Chesapeake Bay Seafood." On January 2nd of that year, the Dayton Ohio Journal Herald ran an article about the violence. "Not all these stories are of ancient vintage," the article stated. "It has been only a few years since a Virginia menhaden fleet pursued a school of fish into Maryland waters and were chased back by the Maryland oyster navy."

The final battle of the Oyster Wars took place in 1959, when an officer shot and killed an illegal dredger from Virginia. Fishery police were thereafter disarmed by Potomac River Fisheries Commissioner H. C. Byrd. No longer would enforcement escalate to bloodshed.

Latrobe's book includes 27 preparations for oysters and 28 for crab,
along with recipes for terrapin, clams, shrimp, lobster, and an assortment
of fish. "Celeried Oysters" is a preparation of butter-sautéed oysters and
celery served on toast. Latrobe accents his recipe with a splash of Sherry.

Celery has a storied history in its own right. Although celery had been grown
since colonial times, it came into fashion in the Victorian Era. New cultivars
put crisp crunch front and center, and made the herb-cum-vegetable easier to
grow.

Sophisticated tables of the late 1800s were accented with purpose-made
celery vases, showcasing the raw stalks in all their glory, ready to be salted and
snacked upon.

Celery and oysters were both enjoying space on the tables of Baltimore's elite
when Ferdinand Latrobe's father, Ferdinand Latrobe Sr., served his multiple
nonconsecutive terms as Baltimore mayor.

Latrobe Sr. ascended in politics in a time when the B&O railroad was building
a wealthy upper class in Baltimore. Latrobe was among them, serving as a
lawyer for the company. His first term as mayor encompassed violent railroad
strikes in which the riot act was invoked. It was just another in the city's long
tradition of violent rioting. Latrobe also oversaw advances in public health,
modernization of infrastructure, and beautification of parks and public places.
When he ran for the mayoral office a fourth time, with a popular song to pro-
pel his notoriety, the "Old Gray Mare" won office handily — and an additional
term after. The campaign song has lasted even longer than his political career.
Celery meanwhile, descended from a de rigueur centerpiece to a diet cliché,
famed for its "negative calories" or reduced to a vehicle for dips and peanut
butter. Thanks to farmers markets where dark green celery makes a seasonal
appearance, it is quietly making its way back to a fashionable table near you.

Dust off that celery vase.

⬛ CELERIED OYSTERS ⬛

Saute 1 pint of Oysters with 1 tablespoon chopped celery, salt and pepper,
in about 2 tablespoons Butter. As you take them from the fire, add 1 glass of
Sherry. Serve on Toast.

recipe from "Chesapeake Bay Seafood," Ferdinand Latrobe, 1940

ꞏ✦Mint Julep✦ꞏ

Josiah Lee
1799-1852
Section A, plot 23

During the lifetime of Josiah Lee, banking was a volatile and unregulated enterprise. Lee must have been concerned when, in 1835, thousands of Baltimore citizens rioted in response to losing their savings at the Bank of Maryland. Circulars were distributed denouncing banks in general. The men involved in the scandal were named and threatened. Lee was not among them, but it was a riotous time in the city. The Baltimore Bank Riot has been called "one of the most violent and destructive events of civic unrest in any American city prior to the Civil War."

The facts on Josiah Lee's life are scant. Perhaps *Lee's Lottery, Exchange, and Stock Office* was so above board and solvent that he didn't have to worry about losing his clients' money. He was a financier of the Baltimore & Ohio railroad, which netted a large profit for many investors in Baltimore. He also published "Lee's Commercial & Literary Gazette," a small newspaper full of odds and ends, mostly reprinted from other publications.

1825 editions of "Lee's Commercial & Literary Gazette" include articles on fashion, world news, selected poetry, essays on topics such as "the importance of the Sabbath," marriage and death announcements, notices of known counterfeit bills, and lists of winning lottery numbers, whose tickets could be redeemed at Lee's offices at the southeast corner of Calvert & Market Streets. Articles within Lee's paper also hinted at the growing tension between the northern and southern states. Like many wealthy Marylanders, Lee was likely to have identified with Southern causes. His Mint Julep recipe appeared in "Recipes Old & New," an 1898 cookbook produced in tandem with the "Confederate Relief Bazaar."

Josiah Lee himself died before the Civil War, in 1852. His banking partners ran an ad assuring the public that his death would "cause no change whatever" in Josiah Lee & Co. business relations.

As his estate was settled in the months after his death, newspapers around the country reported on the sale of the spirits collection of Josiah Lee. His wines and liquors netted $14,000, today's equivalent of a half-million dollars. Colonel John Eager Howard spent $16.50 on a demijohn of Madeira that had belonged to Thomas Jefferson. Twenty-three half-gallon bottles of Rye sold for $4 per bottle. Three demijohns of Cognac, imported in 1804, sold for $11 per gallon.

With such a renowned taste in liquor, it is fitting that his recipes in "Recipes Old & New" were for Brandied Peaches, Noyeau cordial (made with peach kernels), Apple Toddy, and Mint Julep.

Apple Toddy is a historic drink, served (cold) around the holidays. In its day it was a competitor to eggnog, at least in Maryland. But Mint Julep was not without its share of Maryland associations.

In "The News" of Frederick Maryland in 1901, Senator William B. Peter of Howard County provided a recipe for the "real thing": the Maryland Mint Julep.

"Like the Maryland terrapin, the Maryland julep is very simply prepared," he declared. Peter recommended the beverage be made in silver pitchers if possible, even a "silver loving cup" when "the party is such that it is not averse to drinking out of the same vessel."

Mint stems, which impart a bitter flavor, are to be removed, and the leaves steeped in whiskey overnight. No quantity is specified but Peter advised against bruising the leaves. "Fill your loving cup almost to the brim with ice about the size of a small hickory nut, not smaller or larger. Dissolve a-half a dozen lumps of sugar in as little water as possible. Don't use too much sugar; about half a lump to the drink is all you need. Then first pour the sugared water over the ice and follow it with the whiskey, in which the leaves have been steeped but strained off." The drink is stirred and garnished with additional mint sprigs.

In 1909, H. L. Mencken anonymously opined at length on mint juleps in the pages of the Baltimore Sun. Among his sins were using "horse mint" instead of "real green mint", using "artificial ice" —as in ice not harvested from a spring— and using Rye Whiskey. Despite Maryland's association with Rye, Bourbon was the preference.

Josiah Lee's recipe is actually more of an afterthought to a cordial version made with brandy. He specified that it is a good cure for seasickness. It is likely that Lee's recipes made it into the "Recipes Old & New" cookbook via his daughter Mary Catherine Lee, who was married to a relative of the cookbook's compiler, Mrs. Charles Marshall, of Maryland's well-known Snowden family.

Maryland maintained a standing of Mint Julep authority well into the 20th century, but as usual, there was disagreement on how exactly one should be made. In 1933, Maryland senator Millard Tydings contradicted Mencken and called for Rye. Tydings also liked to muddle his mint leaves and sugar together. He did offer one piece of advice that most julep aficionados might agree on: "The genuine Maryland mint julep should be imbibed while leaning forward, telling a good story or while leaning back listening to a good story. This improves the flavor immensely."

MINT CORDIAL OR JULEP

In five gallons of brandy put as much spear mint (picked when the dew is on it) as can be pressed in without bruising. Let them remain together twenty-four hours. Put into a vessel sixteen and one-fourth pounds loaf sugar, on which put the bulk of five gallons in good clear ice, or three gallons of ice water. Pour the brandy from the mint and mix the sugar and water with it. This makes a delicious cordial and when mixed with ice will make a julep superior to that made with fresh mint. It greatly improves with age. Two-thirds of a gill of new milk will clarify that quantity of cordial. For making whiskey julep: two and three-fourth pounds of sugar are required for each gallon of whiskey. (P.S.—This is excellent for *mal de mer*.)

recipe from "Recipes Old and New, Collected by Mrs. Charles Marshall for the benefit of the Confederate relief bazaar," 1898

17

 Caramels

(a.k.a. Fudge)

Alice Whitridge Thomas
1846-1918
Chapel Area, plot 67

The prevailing fudge origin story centers around a Vassar student, Emelyn Hartridge, who popularized the confection on campus; it then spread to other schools. Fudge-making remained associated with women's colleges for decades. Hartridge, it turns out, is said to have gotten the recipe from a schoolmate's cousin in Baltimore. (That's how recipes go, especially sweet ones.)

By 1903, recipes appeared in regional newspapers for "Baltimore Fudge." The women's magazine The Delineator in 1907 referred to "...Baltimore caramels, a confection afterwards known as 'January Thaw' and now called 'fudge.'"

The "January Thaw" term is a little hard to search, but it doesn't seem to have been as prevalent in old newspapers and cookbooks as "Baltimore Fudge" or "Baltimore Caramels."

An early version of the "Caramels" fudge formula appeared in the 1870 Maryland cookbook "Queen of the Kitchen," by Mrs. M.L. Tyson

After appearing in "Queen of the Kitchen," the chocolate caramels recipe was subsequently printed in the classic "Fifty Years in a Maryland Kitchen," by Mrs. B. C. Howard in 1873. Mrs. Charles H. Gibson also included it in her 1894 "Maryland and Virginia Cook Book." In fact, that book includes SEVEN slight variations on the recipe. This made me decide that Mrs. Gibson is kind of irritating.

The recipe appearing on one of the many loose scraps in the late-1800's "Thomas Family Cookbook" has the same ingredients as other recipes, but the quantities are different. The two Thomas recipe books contain recipes handed down through generations, but the primary author is probably Alice Whitridge Thomas, who lived from 1846 to 1918.

Alice's husband, Douglas Hamilton Thomas, was the son of Dr. John Hanson Thomas who lived in the home now known as Hackerman House in Mt. Vernon. Alice's sister Olivia Whitridge, who died in 1851 at the age of nine, has the distinction of being the first person buried at Green Mount.

Buried next to Olivia is Martha Ann "Patty" Atavis, a woman who was enslaved by the Whitridge family. Her image was captured in two surviving tintypes, offering a rare glimpse at the humanity of one of the many people who were enslaved in service of these wealthy families' lifestyles.

Sybby Grant is another enslaved woman connected with the family. In addition to a letter that she wrote to John Hanson Thomas, Sybby's legacy is enshrined in the family recipe books, where a recipe for stewed kidneys is attributed to her.

Not much else is known about Sybby's life, but an 1899 death certificate for 'Syppe Grant,' a 78-year-old Black woman born in Virginia may offer a clue. If this is the same woman, she was buried in Laurel Cemetery, a Black counterpart to Green Mount that was controversially demolished to make way for a shopping center.

The Thomas recipe books contain many Baltimore specialties, including terrapin, Maryland beaten biscuits, and hominy. A number of the recipes are attributed to other Baltimore people, including an eggnog formula that passed through Mrs. George Hawkins Williams to Mrs. Charlotte Smith to Mrs. Douglas H. Thomas— all of whom are buried at Green Mount. The eggnog almost didn't circulate at all. Written on the back is the admonition: "I am shocked to see the way you are spending the Sabbath & I am not going to give you my receipt again."

Other recipes, attributed to only first names like "Henrietta" or "Louisa" may have come from people enslaved or employed by the Thomases or their circle of friends.

Dr. John Hanson Thomas was imprisoned during the civil war for being a — shocker— Confederate sympathizer. During this time, his wife Annie wrote to him every day. These letters offer a look into the casual attitudes typical of enslavers like the Thomases. They seemed to be truly convinced that women like Sybby benefited from having their freedom taken away, and that the Confederate cause had widespread sympathy across racial and geographical lines.

Interspersed right along with these wartime sentiments is the minutiae of the life and times of the family, from preferred seating in church and gossip about someone dying her hair, to the exchange of food gifts including grapes, celery, and cream.

Caramel is mentioned at least once - made by a visitor named Nannie Howard. Could this recipe have come from her? The recipe is a loose scrap in a strange handwriting. Sweet recipes make the rounds.

The Thomas recipe collection serves as a reminder of the wide range of personal contributions to even a personal recipe manuscript. Their vast collection of letters and personal papers provide insights into the connections held within the recipe book, in their uncomfortable complexity.

CARAMELS

¼ pound of chocolate
½ pound of sugar
small piece of butter - size of an egg
½ cup of cream
1 tablespoonful of vanilla
Boil twenty minutes

recipe from Thomas Family Recipe Book. Special Collections and University Archives, Virginia Tech

and let it cook on top of range. Shape
it like an omelet. Turn it over until quite
baked.   Annie's Receipt.

Stewed Kidneys

Cut a beef kidney in small pieces after
having first carefully removed all the fat
&c. Parboil & strain through a cullender.
Skim the water in which the kidneys
have been parboiled & pour into a saucepan
to which add the parboiled kidneys, butter
size of hens egg, pepper & salt three to four
onions chopped up and a little thickening
of browned flour or sugar. Stew for about
20 minutes.   Sitter Grant's recipe

Stewed Kidneys

Wash kidneys in cold water take out all the
gristle & then cut them up adding onion
& plenty of black pepper, place in a
covered vessel & allow them to remain
over night. Cook in the morning
for at least two hours, after stewing
hour & half Rub up small quantity of
flour & butter adding some of the
liquor from the kidney & stir up with
the kidneys then cooking.

Kidneys "à la Lloyd"

21

❧Soft Shell Crab❧

Charles A. Vogeler
1851-1882
Yew Area, plot 10.5

In a time when the lady of the house often doubled as the family doctor, cookbooks were filled with remedies as well as culinary recipes. In the case of German immigrant Charles Vogeler's 1896 recipe book, the cookbook was also a venue for advertisements of patent medicines.

The 35-page booklet devotes roughly half its space to advertisements. St. Jacob's Oil, a pain remedy, is the flagship product advertised throughout. There is an ad for "Hamburg Drops, the great German blood purifier," which could cure indigestion, skin disease, "some types of Female Complaints," "impure blood," and liver ailments. A bottle of the drops in the Smithsonian National Museum of American History's Patent Medicine Collection lists the main ingredient as alcohol.

I'm not sure what was the active ingredient in "Demelvo," a facial hair remover marketed to women. It is listed as "a fragrant liquid compound entirely free from all poisonous ingredients". Women could further beautify themselves with "Klettenwurzel Oel" aka Burdock Root Oil, brushed through the hair to encourage growth and cure dandruff. "Hamburg Plaster" ointment pledged to cure ulcers, burns, cuts, itch, pimples and frostbite.

"Hamburg Breast Tea" soothed coughs, asthma, sore throat, influenza, and other lung concerns. The remedy was used by "every German family in the United States," according to the ad, and was quickly "gaining friends among American families, particularly among the old and feeble."

An ad for Demelvo stated:

"Many beautiful faces are marred by growths of disgusting hair, and doubtless a majority of ladies so afflicted endure painful embarrassment rather than use any preparation for the removal of such blemishes because of their fear of injurious results. Demelvo, A fragrant liquid compound—entirely free from all poisonous ingredients, quickly removes superfluous hair."

But it was St. Jacob's Oil that promised, page after page, to cure toothaches, rheumatism, aches, pains, bruises, sciatica, and more. In an ad towards the back of the book St. Jacob's Oil is recommended "for man and beast!" to heal injuries in horses and maladies of cattle, sheep, swine and poultry. "Full directions for use in eleven languages are enwrapped with every bottle."

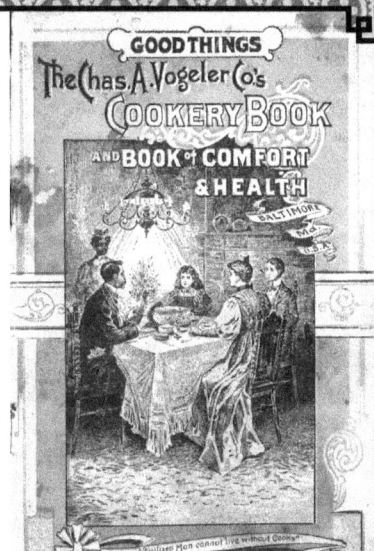

Various sources described St. Jacob's Oil as a mixture of camphor, ether, alcohol, and capsicum, giving a cooling and heating effect. The ointment may have contained aconite root, which can in fact decrease pain— but can also potentially kill you.

Born in Germany in 1819, August Vogeler moved to Baltimore in 1839 and worked for a local drug company. The passenger manifest for the Clementine, the ship he arrived on listed the 21-year-old Vogeler's trade as apothecary.

In 1845, he went into the drugstore business for himself, and eventually formed a partnership in a cough syrup company. In 1876 he formed a second partnership with his son Charles A. Vogeler and John Winkleman. The family produced St. Jacobs Oil, which was a runaway success.

August returned to visit Germany several times, as did Charles, and his son Charles A. The Vogelers may have been doing research for more products to add to their offerings.

The recipe pages in the Vogeler book cover a wide range of dishes including: potato rolls, corn cakes, noodles for soup, asparagus soup, calves' feet soup with poached eggs, soft shell crabs, deviled crabs, stewed eels, braised beef, fried pigs feet, chicken croquettes, fried tripe, curried chicken pie, home-made sausage, celery au gratin, stewed sweet potatoes, fried cucumbers, potato salad, shrimp salad, peach ice cream, pumpkin pie, peach shortcake, coconut cake, huckleberry cake, doughnuts, Cafe au Lait Cake, stuffed [deviled & fried] eggs, fried bananas, iced coffee, and butterscotch candy.

MEAT —Continued.

Broil
split d
clear fi
are do
a dripp
sauce
spoonf
ful of
vinega
fine cr
upper
Transfe
little o
breast

Chic
of cold
can of
mashed
two egg
butter,
drippin
very fi
son. B
and sti
tered fr
quickly
fine cra
nice fat

A frequent use of vinegar aligns with the Vogeler family's German heritage. The recipes are often well-seasoned. The fried pigs' feet are rubbed with mustard and pepper underneath their breading. Broiled chickens are seasoned with mustard, vinegar and cayenne pepper.

The book states that the recipes were written for the Charles A. Vogeler company by "a leading authority." Promotional cookbooks like the Vogeler book often copied recipes wholesale from other sources. Many of the recipes including the fried cucumbers, "Cousin Melissa's Sponge Cake," fried tripe, and curried chicken pie trace to cookbook author and novelist Marion Harland. Harland had a Deviled Crab recipe in her 1873 book "Common sense in the household," but the recipe in The Chas. A. Vogeler Co.'s Cookery Book came from somewhere else, as did the recipe for soft-shell crab. The latter appeared in newspapers around the country at least a decade before the Vogeler cookbook, however. Soft-Shell Crab recipes appear infrequently in older cookbooks, and the fact that Vogeler included one at all is an indication of the assimilation of German immigrants like the Vogeler family into Baltimore's culinary culture.

St. Jacob's oil was apparently marketed as late as the 1940s, although its wild cure-all claims had been reigned in by the Pure Food and Drug Act.

Demelvo seems to have hung around until around 1914. As antique dealers and archaeologists in the region can tell you, many glass bottles that once contained St. Jacob's Oil survived well into the next century. Luckily, they are empty.

Klettenwurzel Oel

(BURDOCK ROOT OIL)

INCREASES THE GROWTH, BEAUTIFIES AND PRESERVES

THE HAIR.

Purely vegetable, it proves to be a **natural invigorator** to the roots of the hair, gives tone and vitality to the surface of the scalp, **removes dandruff** and prevents the loss and **turning gray** of the hair. It gives a rich lustre and softness of texture and is curative of such diseases as often afflict the scalp. In its restorative action it produces a **luxuriant growth.**

24

SOLD BY DRUGGISTS AND DEALERS.
PRICE 50 CENTS, OR FIVE BOTTLES FOR $2.00.

St. Jacobs Oil

THE GREAT REMEDY for PAIN

IT CONQUERS PAIN!

CURES

**RHEUMATISM,
NEURALGIA,
SCIATICA,
LUMBAGO,
SPRAINS, BRUISES,
STIFFNESS,**

▶ SOFT SHELL CRAB ◀

Pull off the spongy parts on the back, under the sides of the shell and from the lower sides of the body. Wash and wipe the crabs, dip in raw beaten egg, then in fine crumbs, and fry in hot salted lard about ten minutes. Drain off the fat, lay on a heated platter, garnish with parsley and send around lemons cut into eighths with them, also cayenne pepper.

recipe from "The Chas. A. Vogeler Co's Cookery Book", Charles A. Vogeler Company, 1896

LERS

CO.
BALTIMORE, Md.

Compliments of

✺❀Corn Pone❀✺

Mrs. James H. Preston
1874-1933
North West Area, plot 71

Colonial Maryland was built on tobacco, but its fuel was corn. Early plant-ers with dollar signs in their eyes were so apt to cover their claimed lands in tobacco crops that Maryland took a cue from Virginia and passed a statute that every person planting tobacco must plant two acres of corn. "Corn" at this time could mean wheat, oats or, well, corn, depending on where you were. In Maryland it meant corn, and the crop has outlasted tobacco as an economic driver of the state's agriculture. Whether its grown for animal feed or to be eaten off the cob like our beloved summer Silver Queen, cornfields as far as the eye can see remain a defining feature of Maryland's landscape.

There are plentiful old recipes for corn fritters (often considered to be an im-itation of oysters), hominy, and cornbread. One recipe that pops up now and then is a greasy and unleavened old-fashioned corn pone.

Helen Fiske Jackson hailed from a prominent family on Maryland's Eastern Shore, and it is possible that the corn pone recipe she contributed to "Eat, Drink & Be Merry in Maryland" is quite old, although the baking soda would not have made its way in there until the 1800s.

Born in 1874 in Salisbury, Helen married James Henry Preston in 1894. Mrs. Pres-ton appeared in the society pages often, for hosting events for debutantes, bridge club, lawn parties, and taking trips to Atlantic City. In 1910, a party held by the Prestons was reported in the Sun with curiosity. At their home at 815 North Charles Street, they hosted an oyster roast "while a band of colored musicians played lively plantation melodies."

"A long table set in the middle of the

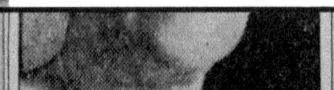

room was decorated with a center-piece of vegetables and ablaze with many tall white candles... Strings of spinach and huge cabbages filled with celery imbedded in crushed ice ornamented the four corners of the table and the china and silverware were of the kitchen variety. At each place was a card of butchers brown paper with an appropriate verse and the name of the guest. Boutonnieres of radishes and parsley for the men and carrots and parsley for the women were at each plate beside a napkin of checked tea toweling."

After dinner, guests participated in an old folk dance called the Virginia Reel.

A little over a year later, Mrs. Preston attended another party: her husband's inauguration as Mayor of Baltimore. James H. Preston spoke of bringing more factories to Baltimore, and keeping the city "free from graft." He outlined his plans for mayorship.

Ultimately, James H. Preston's contribution would be as one of the architects of Baltimore's racial segregation. To this day, his name lives on in a downtown park whose ostensible purpose was to beautify

MRS. JAMES H. PRESTON

and clear a "slum." It was in actuality a thriving Black neighborhood. The use of land condemnation and "slum clearance" officially entered the toolbox of segregationists.

Another of Preston's pet projects lives on. In 1914 he dedicated much energy to the "Star-Spangled Banner Centennial," emphasizing Baltimore's role in the national anthem. Five years later, a "Report of the City Officers and Departments" documented praise for Mayor James H. Preston for devoting his "time and ability" for the planning of the celebration which "reflected the

Dies At Her Home
After Month's Illness

MRS. J. PRESTON
DIES AT HER HOME

Mr. And Mrs. James H. Preston
Unique Entertainment

greatest credit upon the people of Baltimore and.. also brought our City of Baltimore to the attention of the world in a way most gratifying to all Baltimoreans..." In light of the continuing pride that Baltimore takes in all things "Star Spangled," this event has had a lasting impact.

Life as Baltimore's first lady would put Helen in contact with the wives of men like William Jennings Bryan and Randolph Hearst. Her 1933 obituary referred to her as "Lady Mayoress" and said she was known for her "liberal views," such as "a woman's morality is not to be judged by the number of petticoats she does or does not wear" and defending the tango from being banned by clergy. During James Preston's unsuccessful 1923 campaign, she spoke to the newspaper of plans to "sprinkle" city streets to keep down dust, "kill the mosquito" and beautify Baltimore. She urged women to vote, and ended the interview with some enthusiastic declarations: "I think that this is a wonderful world! It's a pleasure to be alive! Music to me is wonderful—I never get enough of good music."

She may have defended the tango and had a zest for life, but Helen Preston was an active participant in the political campaigning of a man who once refused to shake hands with Black students at their graduation that he attended. Aside from the named vestiges in Baltimore, there may not be much to remember Mayor James H. Preston by, but his legacy is still evoked whenever land deals in the city purposely or unwittingly displace Black residents. The park is an interesting space downtown. Preston had hoped it would be "a place to congregate, reflect and admire beauty." Perhaps it is a place to reflect on the mistakes of the past.

CORN PONE

Three eggs, one teaspoon of sugar, one cup of melted shortening (lard - roast beef or chicken fat), two cups of buttermilk, scant teaspoon of soda, three cups of corn meal. Sift dry ingredients together, beat eggs and sugar together, add milk and meal, lastly pour in the shortening. Bake in a hot oven fifteen or twenty minutes.

recipe from "Eat, Drink, and Be Merry in Maryland," Frederick Philip Stieff, 1932.

"The Wonderful Human Flag"
COMPOSED OF SIXTY-FIVE HUNDRED SCHOOL CHILDREN, PRODUCED AT FORT McHENRY, SEPTEMBER 12, 1914.

This is to Certify that _____
was a member of the "Human Flag" as above depicted.

James H. Preston
Mayor

Compliments of The Municipal Journal, Baltimore, Md., A. S. Goldsborough, Managing Editor.

29

Tomato "Catsup"

Mabel Roberts
1880-1959
Sycamore Area, plot 45

The cookbook boom of the 1800s had publishers eager to print recipe books with a range of themes. Some were regional, some health or budget oriented, while others touted the emerging field of cooking science or capitalized on a semi-famous author.

A publisher and stationer in Baltimore, Cushings & Bailey, observed the market for a different kind of cookbook: a blank one.

Old recipe manuscripts were often written in blank notebooks, loose pages bound together, or with recipes pasted on top of old ledgers or school workbooks. Cushings & Bailey entitled their product "The Housekeeper's Casket and Cook's Delight," which is stamped across the front cover. The book declared itself to be "the only scientific and perfect form of book for preservation of recipes ever made." (Sometimes I get the distinct feeling that manufacturers historically have not had a high estimation of the intelligence of women but then again maybe it was consumers in general.)

The "Housekeeper's Casket and Cook's Delight" has the same shortcomings as many blank recipe books: sections labeled "soups," "meats," "fish," etc., each with an equal amount of dedicated empty pages.

Some of those sections were left entirely blank in a copy of this book now held at the Maryland Center for History and Culture. The name "Mabel Roberts" is written on the inside cover, but there are several handwritings found in the book. This is fairly common as recipe books were often passed through families or generations.

My best guess at the identity of the "Mabel Roberts" who contributed to this particular recipe manuscript is Mabel Junkins, born in 1880 to Joseph William Junkins and Alice V. Davis.

Originally from Maine, J. Wm. Junkins was a pickle manufacturer during the time when canneries abounded in Baltimore City. The Junkins cannery occupied most of the 1900 block of East Hoffman Street, northeast of Johns Hopkins hospital. The "J. Wm. Junkins" name appears in catalogs for collectors of antique bottles, and worthpoint.com has pictures of an old catsup bottle.

One of the recipes inside the "Housekeeper's Casket and Cook's Delight" is for pickles, and another for "Tomato 'Catsup'." Preserving recipes are in the minority, however. Most of the rest are for cakes and desserts, which is fairly typical of the era. Then as now, a lot of recipes were copied down for the very idea of something the author might like to eat. Others are definitely from family, attributed to "Mama," "Auntie," and "Aunt Soph."

Typical to 19th century recipe books, there are also a number of household remedies and cleaning aids, for indigestion, warts, dandruff, freckles, insect bites and more. Management of these maladies fell on the lady of the house along with the cooking.

Two of the recipes - for fried sea bass and remoulade sauce, are attributed to the Mount Washington Hotel in Bretton Woods New Hampshire, a relic of a vacation at the grand hotel some time in the early 1900s.

Even if my suspicions are correct and this Mabel Roberts is the book's author, it is unlikely that the pickle and catsup formulas bear much resemblance to the industrial products produced by Junkins' company.

Like so many factories lost to time, there is not much information about how J Wm. Junkins got into the canning business or what his products were like. His 1914 Baltimore Sun obituary referred to him as "a pioneering preserving man of this city." On his death, the company ceased and supplies were sold off, including horses, wagons, kettles, pulleys, scales, a gasoline engine, "and the balance of the stock of pickles." Within those pickles was the last of the Junkins product that the world would ever taste.

Plum=Pudding

▶ TOMATO CATSUP ◀

Wash & cut the tomatoes & boil until they can be mashed through a colander then mashed or rather strained through a sieve.

To every gallon of juice thus obtained add 1 pound of brown sugar - 4 Tablespoons salt, 3 Tablespoons Black pepper, 3 Tablespoons mustard (well mixed first with a little of the juice), 1 Tablespoon ginger, 1/2 Tablespoon spice, 1/2 cup celery seed, 1 pint vinegar, 1 pint chopped onions. Thoroughly mix all the spices and sift in, and well mix all together & bottle & seal while hot.

recipe from "Cook Book, n.d.," MS 563, H. Furlong Baldwin Library.

WM. JÜNKIN
CATSUP
BALTIMORE
MD.

the milk - Stir in gradually the bread Crumbs (grated) then the sugar & next the suet & fruit. After this has been mixed ... & last of all the ... and dont fo... ... with ... your "Puddin... boiling ... inside ... in yo... puddin... ...for Swelli... up - be sure to tie it up tight - *Boil Constantly for six hours*

* Mix this 1/2 pound Flour well into the batter before putting into the bag

32

Beneath these rugged oaks, that elm tree's shade,
   Where heaves the turf in many a mouldering heap,
Each in his narrow cell forever laid,
   The rude forefathers of the hamlet sleep.

Can storied urn or animated bust,
   Back to its mansion call the fleeting breath,
Can honor's voice provoke the silent dust
   Or flattery soothe the dull, cold ear of death.

The boast of heraldry, the pomp of power,
   And all that beauty, all that earth ere gave,
Await alike the inevitable hour,
   The paths of glory lead but to the grave.

One morn I missed him on the accustomed hill
   Along the heath, and near his favorite tree,
Another came—nor yet beside the rill,
   Nor up the lawn, nor at the wood was he.

The next, with dirges due, and sad array,
   Slow through the churchway path we saw him bourne
Approach and read, for thou can'st read the lay,

Graved on the stone beneath yon aged thorn.

ᴖ⧫Kossuth Cakes⧫ᴖ

Mrs. George Ray Hyde
1888-1986
Section X, plot 88

In the 1800s, a visit from a touring celebrity could stir an American city into a frenzy. Baltimore was no exception. Whether it was an American Revolutionary like Marquis de Lafayette or an opera star like Jenny Lind, the local papers would load up on coverage, businesses would cash in, and crowds thronged around arriving trains, hoping to get a glimpse of fame. Both Lafayette's 1824 visit and Jenny Lind's in 1850 resulted in cake recipes named in their honor. They can occasionally be found in old cookbooks and recipe manuscripts.

The high-profile visit of Lajos Kossuth resulted in a dessert with a bit more endurance. The Hungarian revolutionary received a hero's welcome when he landed in New York in December of 1851. Newspapers all over the country reported his activities as he traveled from city to city. Men began to emulate Kossuth's hat and beard. A county in Iowa was named in his honor, as was a street in Baltimore. A search of census records reveals babies born in 1852 named Kossuth. He was an icon.

On his way to Washington DC, Kossuth accepted an invitation to visit Baltimore, where he was entertained by the well-to-do.

Among the elites Kossuth visited in Baltimore were the Thomas family. According to Baltimore Sun writer John Dorsey, "It was in Mrs. Thomas's kitchen that the first Kossuth cakes were made in Baltimore." Though the article mistakenly described Kossuth as Polish, the story itself seems plausible.

Enslaved cook Sibby Grant would have been working in the kitchen of the Thomas home at this time, but probably not alone. It is possible that they had a pastry chef. Allegedly, Kossuth described a favorite pastry and Mrs. Thomas had it recreated for him. The resulting dessert started a craze — a piece of the famous nobleman that even people who didn't have a new baby to name could get in on.

An analysis of Kossuth Cakes compared to Hungarian pastries reveals a resemblance to Hungarian Cream Puffs, also known as "Indianerkrapfen" i.e. "Indian Cakes" or "Moors Head" cakes. There are various fantastical stories about

With the Razing of Evesham, Another Bit of Old Baltimore Will Go

their origin, involving a desperate theater manager and one or more magicians from India, but the name could also be some weird racist reference. Kossuth Cakes were celebrated in Francis F. F. Beirne's 1951 book "The Amiable Baltimoreans" but were largely forgotten by that point. When the Hammond-Harwood House compiled a fund-raising cookbook called "Maryland's Way" in 1963, it was the first time, to my knowledge, that a recipe for Kossuth Cakes had been printed in a Maryland cookbook since the 1870s. Bakeries hadn't advertised them for sale in the Baltimore newspapers in several decades.

Mrs. George Ray Hyde, born Henrietta Clemens in 1888, was not alive for Kossuth's legendary visit, but probably enjoyed his namesake cakes from Baltimore bakeries during her childhood.

Henrietta's father Augustus Ducas Clemens Jr. was a prominent "real estate man" in Baltimore, developing areas around Waverly and Govans. In 1895 he purchased Evesham, the onetime home of Betsy Bonaparte Patterson's niece Caroline.

In 1912, "Retta" married George Ray Hyde, treasurer of his father's chain of downtown lunch rooms that had once been known as "The Millionaires Club" for their popularity with bankers. One location was 205 West Fayette Street which as of this writing, is still standing.

When George's father George Washington Hyde died in 1931, the restaurants were closed and the younger George went into real estate.

The Hydes lived at Evesham with the Clemenses and assorted other family. The mansion had 23 rooms and sat on 80 acres. During the Great Depression, the acres dwindled as they were sold off for development.

When George Ray Hyde died in 1952, Retta was left with Evesham and it was more than she could handle. She sold the home she loved and moved to Gibson Island. The Hydes' son Bryden Bordley Hyde was an architect who had worked on preservation projects and designed a floor of the Baltimore Museum of Art. With Bryden's help, stairways and flooring, fireplaces, windows and more were salvaged from Evesham and incorporated into the new home. Other elements like ceiling panels were meticulously duplicated.

One element, stained glass panels depicting ships and trains, was said to have been removed from the famous Barnum's Hotel in Baltimore, which Retta's father purchased and razed in the 1890s. At Gibson Island, Bryden

This stairway, too, will be used in the Gibson Island dwelling Mrs. Hyde's son, Bryden Bordley Hyde, an architect, has desig

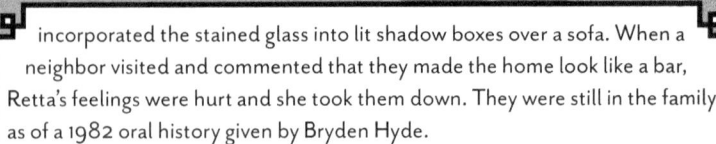

incorporated the stained glass into lit shadow boxes over a sofa. When a neighbor visited and commented that they made the home look like a bar, Retta's feelings were hurt and she took them down. They were still in the family as of a 1982 oral history given by Bryden Hyde.

In that oral history, the Hyde son doesn't mention much about food or eating, but he does mention that the family employed Black cooks, revealing another possible way that the Kossuth Cake recipe made its way to Retta.

Lajos Kossuth's visit to America was a failure by his own standards. He'd intended on raising capital towards his cause. While he collected money from merchandise and appearance fees, it was only a fraction of what he'd hoped to leave with.

Kossuth's unsuccessful fundraising became a legend sold alongside his namesake confection. When Mrs. George Ray Hyde's recipe for Kossuth Cakes appeared in "Maryland's Way," the story was printed beneath the recipe. "The reception given him was said to have been exceeded in hospitality only by that accorded General Lafayette in 1824. However, in spite of Baltimore's enthusiasm to assist General Kossuth's struggle against tyranny, its monetary contribution amounted to only $25." Kossuth returned to Europe, but Kossuth Cakes remained popular for decades. "It would seem that Baltimore got the best of the bargain."

The cak... scooped in that the whipped cream filling will rest securely between them. Then the tops are coated with their chocolate frosting.

After setting the chocolate tops aside to dry, Mr. Vidali puts th... into their fluted paper cups, and fills them high with whippe...

American Visit of Shrewd Mr. Kossuth

A HUNGARIAN PATRIOT
WHO STIRRED THIS COUNTRY 80 YEARS AGO

by

THOMAS P. BROCKWAY

Hominy Balls

Mrs. J. J. Forbes Shaw
1874-1933
Outline Area 1, plot 63

Hominy has a long history in Maryland and featured prominently among the offerings of Baltimore's industrial canneries at the turn of the 20th century. The hominy industry even inspired an odd spinoff product called Coralline, which was marketed as "superior to all other food." Alas, the product existed for only a few years before the Maryland Hominy and Coralline Company factory burned down.

Today, Manning's Hominy is the last of the Baltimore-canned hominies to survive. Although it is now manufactured in Virginia, Manning's Hominy is a nostalgic tradition for many Baltimoreans.

Recipes like Mrs. J. J. Forbes Shaw's Hominy Balls, aka fritters, were a fun way to use up leftover hominy, but canned hominy works just as well.

Mrs. Shaw contributed this recipe — along with many others, from soups to sweets — to the circa-1920 Tried and True Recipe Book of the Woman's Guild of the Church of St. Michael and All Angels. The cookbook contains many names that sound familiar to Maryland historians: Mosher, Sothoron, Diffen-derfer, etc.

Mrs. Shaw, the wife of a Baltimore banker and tobacco merchant, was not as prominent, but she hailed from well-known families. She was born Harriet Alexander Hereford in Union WV in 1874. Her father, Frank Hereford was a senator and congressman. Her grandfather on her mother's side, Hugh Elm-wood Caperton, was also a congressman. The maternal side of her family were ancestors of William Gaston Caperton III, the governor of West Virginia from 1989-1997.

Harriet married James John Forbes Shaw in 1907, and the family lived at 1809 N. Calvert Street. They were fairly notable citizens, turning up in society columns in the Sun. In 1921, however, their mentions took a turn for the tragic. Their 12-year old daughter Alice Caperton Shaw drowned when a rowboat containing the girl, her two sisters, and three other children capsized on the Severn River. Reverend Wyatt-Brown, whose photo appears in the front of

"The Tried and True Recipe Book," rescued the other five children. The many newspapers that covered the incident reported that he was a nervous wreck after the tragedy, marked with scratches from the children's grasps. Twelve years after the harrowing incident, in April 1933, Harriet Shaw died at age 59. Mr. Shaw did not recover from the pain of these deaths. On September 20th, 1937, he visited the graves of his wife and daughter at Green Mount Cemetery. Eventually, he kneeled on the ground, pulled out a pistol and took his own life. The cemetery superintendent who had been watching Shaw pace in the cemetery cried out, but it was too late. Shaw left a note pinned to his clothing, stating simply "The act is my own."

The Shaw home on Calvert Street is no longer standing, but nearby, The Church of St. Michael & All Angels is still there at 2013 St. Paul. The reverend who saved the surviving daughters from the boat accident, Hunter Wyatt-Brown, was known for weaving the "Lost Cause" ideology into his sermons, and Mrs. Shaw had been a member of the Daughters of the Confederacy. Today, The Church of St. Michael & All Angels serves a multicultural congregation.

Although Wyatt-Brown left Maryland to become a bishop in Harrisburg, Pennsylvania, his son Bertram Wyatt-Brown returned to Baltimore to study history at Johns Hopkins. Writing for The Society for U.S. Intellectual History in 2015, Andrew Hartman described Bertram Wyatt-Brown's work: "Bert... zeroed in on the tragic and gothic South, as well as a host of men and women, gnarled by death, humiliation, loss, and anxieties. His books are populated by the chronically depressed, and by tortured writers on the brink of suicide, or novelists who were as much at war with the self as the region they called home."

⟨ HOMINY BALLS ⟩

One pint milk, 1 cup hominy, yolks of 2 eggs, salt and pepper to taste, 1 teaspoon chopped parsley. Cook hominy, then add to milk and cook till thick, beat until smooth, add yolks and cook 10 minutes longer. Take from fire, add parsley and salt and pepper and stand aside to cool. When very cold form into round balls and fry in boiling fat.

recipe from "The Tried and True Recipe Book". Woman's Guild, Church of St. Michael and All Angels. 1920.

⋙Pineapple Sherbert⋘

Charlotte M. Friend
1884-1940
Section O, plot 58

In November 1910, hundreds of women showed up to the Bernheimer Brothers store in downtown Baltimore to enter their bread loaves, biscuits, pies, doughnuts, and cakes to be judged by "representatives of local newspapers." The Baltimore Sun described some cakes as 'ornamental in the extreme' and praised 'the skill shown by Baltimore women,' but did not print the names of the winners or describe their creations.

Perhaps the Sun was inspired by the success of this event to hold its own contest in early 1911.

Newspapers had been having similar contests since the 1890s. In 1901, the San Francisco Examiner used a format similar to the one the Sun would later use: a series of weekly contests in different categories, the recipes delivered to the paper by mail. The winning recipes - including addresses and names of the winners, were printed in lavishly illustrated spreads each week in the Sunday women's pages. The Examiner advertised their contest series as "the biggest thing ever heard of." What newspaper could resist trying to replicate "the biggest thing ever heard of?"

The Sun asked its 1911 readers "Are You A Good Cook?," and offered a $5 prize for the winner, with five one-dollar runner-up awards. The twenty-three weekly contests were judged by Miss Lillian Armstrong, director of the Y.W.C.A. School of Domestic Science. It is unknown whether the recipes were judged by actually tasting them. Around fifty recipes were printed each week, so it doesn't seem likely that Miss Armstrong and company had time to test the entries. Perhaps she used her domestic expertise to envision the recipe results. Over the contest's twenty-three-week run, 1,541 recipes were printed. Several people won repeatedly. Among them was Charlotte M. Friend of 2027 Guilford Avenue, who won a dollar for her Pineapple Sherbet. She also had recipes printed for Orange Marmalade and Martha Washington Crab Soup.

Of Charlotte, I know little. She was one of seven siblings, born in 1884 to Charles and Florence Friend. Charles was a bookstore clerk. Charlotte

never married. Charlotte never married. She followed her slightly older sister Martha into nursing, and together they went overseas during World War I, to England and France. Charlotte was inducted into the Order of St. Sava, for "humanity and gallantry performed under fire."

The Friend family mostly stayed out of the news, except for Charlotte's recipe wins and a 1901 report that Charles was suing Florence for divorce on grounds of adultery. Florence did not contest the lawsuit. When she died in 1906, she was buried with her parents in Mount Olivet Cemetery.

Charlotte was buried in Green Mount, with her father and Martha, who also never married. Although Charlotte Friend left no children, it seems probable that she saved lives in the war. Her legacy may be out there somewhere.

PINEAPPLE SHERBERT

Boil 1 quart of water with 1 pound of granulated sugar, set aside to cool; when cold add juice of 2 lemons and 1 medium-sized pineapple, grated; put into freezer and pack, allow it to stand about 5 minutes so as to become thoroughly chilled, turn until it starts to harden, then add the whites of 2 eggs beaten stiff with 2 tablespoons of powdered sugar, turn for about 10 minutes, remove the dasher and pack carefully; allow to stand for 1/2 hour at least. This fills a 2-quart freezer and is our favorite frozen dessert.

recipe from The Baltimore Sun Recipe Contest, 1911

Huckleberry Fritters

Ida Auld
1869-1925
Beech Area 1, plot 55

In 1877, Frederick Douglass met with Thomas Auld, the man who had enslaved him. Forty years before, Douglass made an escape to Rochester New York, with the aid of his wife Anna Murray, a sailor suit, and faked papers. Auld hired bounty hunters to no avail. One of slavery's greatest foes set on his course to change history.

For all of Douglass' unflinching depictions of the situation in Maryland, on the Eastern Shore where his life began, and in Baltimore from whence he fled, he was not without conflict. His escape went smoothly, but "within there was trouble," he wrote in his 1845 autobiography. " I had a number of warm-hearted friends in Baltimore,--friends that I loved almost as I did my life, --and the thought of being separated from them forever was painful beyond expression." The experience led Douglass to reflect on the cruel conflicts that faced enslaved people. "It is my opinion that thousands would escape from slavery, who now remain, but for the strong cords of affection that bind them to their friends. The thought of leaving my friends was decidedly the most painful thought with which I had to contend."

Frederick Douglass' rational denunciations of the evils of slavery strike the modern reader as apparent truths. It is the humanity within that remains a revelation - the complexity of emotion told honestly from the perspective of someone who'd lived through something almost unimaginable.

When Douglass was moved as a child from the brutal conditions on the Wye Plantation to Baltimore, he encountered something new to him. "It was a white face beaming with the most kindly emotions; it was the face of my new mistress, Sophia Auld." It is important to remember the intended audience for Douglass' memoir. He knew he had to reach the hearts and minds of his white readers. But his relationship with the Auld family unfolded in real life with the unanswerable contradictions of reckoning with dehumanization.

"Going to live at Baltimore laid the foundation, and opened the gateway, to all my subsequent prosperity," he wrote, leaving us forever to consider the fickle conditions that shape our country. Sophia Auld began to teach Frederick Douglass to read. When her husband Hugh Auld found out, he threw a tantrum that is described in detail in "Narrative of the Life of Frederick Douglass, an American Slave, written by Himself." The book can be found online, and the painful interaction is a hard but necessary read. Hugh Auld's words hurt Douglass while also illuminating the depth of self-awareness of the enslaver, intent on suppressing enslaved people from learning despite claims of their inferiority and subservience.

Douglass invoked the Aulds again in 1848 in an open letter to Thomas Auld in which he wrote "I entertain no malice toward you personally. There is no roof under which you would be more safe than mine, and there is nothing in my house which you might need for your comfort, which I would not readily grant...I am your fellow-man, but not your slave." The powerful sentiment lays hypocrisy bare and unsettling.

When he faced Thomas Auld in 1877, Auld had little choice but to repent. "I always knew you were too smart to be a slave," he told Douglass, "and had I been in your place, I should have done as you did."

Douglass had been in touch with Hugh Auld even before the Emancipation Proclamation. In 1857 he wrote the man a letter in which he declared, "I love you, but hate Slavery."

"I have often felt a strong desire to hold a little correspondence with you and to learn something of the position and prospects of your dear children," he wrote. He had been a child himself when he was brought to Baltimore. Among the four Auld children was Benjamin Franklin Auld Sr., who was ten years old when Douglass escaped slavery in 1838. Benjamin Auld became police captain of Baltimore, and had his own son in 1866.

Benjamin Franklin Auld, Jr. did not have a particularly splashy life. According to the census he was a mail carrier. In 1911, his wife, the former Ida Matilda Black, was one of dozens of Baltimore women to "win" a weekly recipe contest. The theme on the week of May 7th was griddle cakes, and Ida Auld shared a recipe for Huckleberry Fritters.

The Aulds' dark history remained part of family lore. In 1925, Ida and Benjamin's son Franklin wrote to the Evening Sun to defend his family's honor after the Reverend George F. Bragg, an early civil rights activist, mentioned Hugh Auld in a public letter. Franklin's letter painted Douglass as unappreciative and ambitious, and his own family as kind and indulgent. The bitter letter is a bleak coda to the story of the Aulds and Douglass, suggesting the futility of reconciliation and forgiving the unforgivable. Immediately beside Auld's letter was a story about the Klan marching in Washington.

There's a lot to unpack in the intricate and puzzling relationships of these people. It's overwhelming to brush up against in just researching the background of a woman and her Huckleberry Fritters. But the fritter recipe is a reminder of the depth of brutal history lurking under the ordinary lives of Baltimoreans in the decades after the Civil War and indeed to this day.

Sophia Auld's grave is in Baltimore Cemetery. On the website findagrave.com, three people have left virtual flowers to her memory. One user wrote to her "Sorry you turned to ungodly wickedness." Another posted the image of the Methodist cross, and the words "May God have mercy upon your soul."

HUCKLEBERRY FRITTERS

Make a batter of 1 pint of flour, 1 teaspoon of baking powder, pinch of salt, 2 well-beaten eggs and 1 pint of milk. Then stir in 1 pint of huckleberries which have been washed and drained. Have lard very hot and drop the batter by spoonfuls in the hot lard. Fry a golden brown and sprinkle with pulverized sugar.

recipe from The Baltimore Sun Recipe Contest, 1911

44

Rochester Oct. 4th 1857

Hugh Auld Esq
  — My dear Sir.

                    My heart tells me that
you are too noble to treat with indifference the
request I am about to make, It is twenty years
since I ranaway from you, or rather not from you
but from Slavery, and since then I have often felt
a strong desire to hold a little correspondence with you
and to learn something of the position and prospects
of your dear children— They were dear to me— and
are still— indeed I feel nothing but kindness for
you all— I love you, but hate Slavery, Now my
dear Sir, will you favor me by dropping me a line, telling
me in what year I came to live with you in Alieeanna st
the year the Frigate was built by Mr. Beacham—
The information is not for publication— and shall
not be published — We are all hastening where all
distinctions are ended, kindness to the humblest will
not be unrewarded
Perhaps you have heard that I have seen Miss Amanda
that was, Mrs Sears that is, and was treated kindly
Such is the fact, Gladly would I see you and Mrs.
Auld— or Miss Sopha as I used to call her.
I could have lived with you during life in freedom
though I ranaway from you so uncerimoniously,
I did not know how soon I might be sold. But I hate
to talk about that, A line from you will find me Addressed Fredk. Douglass
Rochester N. York. I am dear Sir very truly yours. Fred: Douglass

45

Louisiana Ring Cake

Duane H. Rice
1845-1921
Beech Area 1, plot 22

In November of 2024, a reader approached me when I was selling books at the Downtown Farmers' Market. She described her mother's wonderful recipe scrapbook. "She had multiple recipes for Louisiana Ring," she said as I considered mentioning I had no idea what that was. "One recipe is the good one and she put a star beside it." I imagined some type of aspic. I didn't figure it for a Maryland recipe for obvious reasons.

Until one hour later. A stranger came up and chatted me up about beaten biscuits. She used to get them at Graul's, she told me. "They also used to sell this cake," she went on, "called a Louisiana Ring."

As soon as I got home, I searched my database. Sure enough, I had four recipes for the cake. One recipe appeared in the excellent BGE "Maryland Classics" cookbook. A recipe in volume two of "Dining Down Memory Lane" by Shelley Howell is specifically associated with the beloved Rice's Bakery. Another of my recipes was handwritten into blank space in a community cookbook. Clearly, this was a sought-after cake.

Forty years before my encounter, Rose Davis was seeking. In February of 1983, she wrote to a nationally syndicated recipe exchange newspaper column that she'd had "fond memories of a cake she used to buy from Rice's Bakery about 30 years ago. It was an orange-flavored pound cake with a crunchy coating, called 'Louisiana Ring Cake.'" Could anyone find the recipe?

One year later, she received a reply. "C.R." from Miami wrote "I am from New Orleans and have never heard of Louisiana Ring Cake... however, this may be what she wanted. This is a traditional Mardi Gras cake," providing a King Cake recipe. It was a reasonable assumption. But an incorrect one.

Finally, in March 1984, Mrs. Anthony Donnell of Claymont Delaware sent in a cake recipe containing orange and almond extracts, and a crunchy topping. "This looks like the real thing," wrote Nancy Coale Zippe, the column's author. Request solved; discussion ended.

Except in Baltimore.

The memory of the Louisiana Ring Cakes, delivered directly to customers from Rice's Bakery trucks, never faded. In 1986, Evening Sun columnist Gilbert Sandler described a typical delivery from Rice's to his household: "a dozen Parkerhouse rolls, a cherry pie — and a Louisiana Ring Cake."

Sandler interviewed a retired manager of the bakery, Emory Rice Jr., who regaled with the story of how the bakery originally made deliveries by horse and wagon. "Each of our drivers was ally with each housewife," he said. "He'd tell her our specials, she'd tell him what... she had in mind that day. The big favorite, year after year after year, was Rice's Louisiana Ring Cake."

Sandler commented that the original recipe for the cake seemed to be lost. The bakery closed in 1974; the towering Rice's sign over Orleans Street was gone.

One reader, Pat D'Amario, took issue with the statement that the recipe was lost. "I can assure you," she wrote to Sandler, "that the original recipe for Rice's Louisiana Ring Cake is alive and well. My father Eugene Buchler created it." When asked to share the recipe, she smugly replied, "No, that stays in our family."

Curtis Rice and his son Duane founded Rice's Bakery just before the Civil War. Both appear in Baltimore's 1870 census as bakers. An 1882 ad listed three locations for "Rice's Vienna Bakery" and advertised Vienna Bread for Christmas Morning.

Unlike many of Baltimore's other famous bakers, the Rices didn't hail from Germany. For whatever reason, the family came to Baltimore from Vermont, where their family roots went back for many generations.

Eugene Buchler, according to his 1987 obituary, was from Germany, however. He immigrated to Baltimore in the 1940s.

Buchler may have developed a recipe for the cake for his employer, but Louisiana Ring Cake already existed elsewhere by that time. A bakery in Massachusetts advertised the cake in 1937 as "the cake that everybody knows and likes." An ad for "Big Chain Stores" in the Shreveport Louisiana Times in 1939 described an "extra rich pound cake with ground orange and coconut in the batter."

Meanwhile, in Indiana, Freihofer's Bakery in Indianapolis described their Louisiana Ring as "a rich golden ring, flavored only with fresh orange fruit and tender crushed macaroons baked into the top and sides of the cake, covered over with powdered sugar."

Today, different recipes persist for these variations, sometimes under the name "Louisiana Crunch Cake." The only apparent tie to Louisiana, Big Chain aside, seems to be the similarity of the cake's shape to that of a King Cake. Thanks to Rice's, Louisiana Ring Cake became a mainstay in the Baltimore area. The recipes printed in Baltimore newspapers and local community cookbooks are all similar.

I made the cake several times, first attempting to use the recipe hand-written into my copy of "The Best in Cooking in Orangeville," a 1960 Baltimore neighborhood cookbook. That recipe was copied down wrong and missing several ingredients. Most other recipes entail reserving a part of the batter to mix with additional sugar and flavoring and pouring this into the ring pan to make the crust. This works well. The best method I found, however, formed the crunchy crust from some of the mixed dough before adding the eggs and milk. This version of the recipe was shared by Bel Air Branch librarian Jean McLane in the Bel Air Aegis newspaper in 1983. Thank you Jean!

LOUISIANA RING CAKE

2 ¾ Cups flour
2 Teaspoons baking powder
½ Teaspoon salt
1 ¾ Cups sugar
1 Cup butter
¾ Cup milk
1 Teaspoon orange extract
¼ Teaspoon almond extract
3 eggs

Topping:
4 Teaspoons flour
2 Tablespoons powdered sugar
2 Tablespoons brown sugar
½ Teaspoon orange extract

Sift flour, baking powder, salt, and sugar together. Cut in butter. Reserve 1/2 cup of this crumb mix for topping and set aside. Add milk, extracts, and eggs to batter and beat at medium speed for 4 minutes. Next add reserved crumb mix to topping ingredients. Sprinkle topping on bottom of well-greased 9" tube pan. Pour batter on top. Bake at 350°F for 50 to 60 minutes till done. Remove from pan immediately.

Recipe from the Bel Air Aegis, July 7, 1983, shared by Jean McLean

Bill Wilson

RICES!

RICES BAKERY

RICES BAKERY

I REMEMBER MR. WILLIAMS AND THOSE GREAT PIES!

49

⊷Harvey Salad Dressing⊶

Miss Lulie P. Hooper
1875-1955
Chestnut Area 2, plot 26

The 1936 Lovely Lane Cook Book, produced by the historic Methodist church of the same name, brims with "dainty" recipes: Date and Nut Bread; cakes and cookies; ice box rolls; Frozen Banana Salad. There's luncheon dishes and cheese fondue and "Fruit Punch to Serve Ten."

Like many church cookbooks, "Lovely Lane Cook Book" was full of recipes worthy of an elegant ladies' luncheon or a bridge game with tea.

And then there is Lulie Hooper's recipe for "Harvey Salad Dressing." Beef bouillon; chopped olives, blue cheese, garlic, catsup, capers, vinegar, Worcestershire sauce. Hooper's recipe is an umami bomb packed with sodium, acidity, and pungency. Though it seems vaguely Caesar dressing-inspired, it takes things to another level.

It is likely that the dressing name is somehow related to Fred Harvey, a pioneer in railroad cuisine and later purveyor of a chain of restaurants . However, I couldn't find any other version of this recipe among the recipes associated with Harvey.

Miss Lulie Hooper was the granddaughter of Robert Poole, whose family had immigrated to Baltimore from Ireland when he was a child. Poole operated a foundry and machinery shop, relocating it to Woodberry in 1853. With its location near the Northern Central Railway and the area's many textile mills, Poole and his partner German Hunt did good business. The next year, the foundry would produce ironwork for the roof, dome and columns of the U.S. Capital building.

The expansion of the mills and the housing for their workers continued. By the Civil War, Woodberry was the largest industrial town in the state - outside of Baltimore.

In 1888, Baltimore city expanded northward from its North Avenue border to encompass Woodberry and its surroundings. The annexation increased the city's size from ten to thirty square miles.

William E. Hooper had founded the similarly successful Hooper Mills not far from Poole's mills.

In 1871, Hooper's son James Edward Hooper married Robert Poole's daughter Sarah. James Hooper would eventually become the president of the merged Mount Vernon Woodberry Cotton Duck Company. Lulie Poole Hooper was the fourth of their six children.

Born into this wealthy family, Lulie engaged in the typical charitable pursuits of a woman of her class, and joined the Foreign Missionary Society of the Methodist Church, which took her on missionary trips to Asia and the Pacific. She was educated at Goucher College, founded in 1885 by the Methodist church, and with ample funding from the Poole-Hooper family. Lulie graduated in 1896 and remained involved with the college for the rest of her life, eventually having Hooper Hall named in her honor.

Margie Luckett included Lulie Hooper in "Maryland Women," a three-volume collection of biographies of contemporary and historical women of the state. Although most of the women in the books come from obvious wealth, there is no particular political bent to the collection. The activities and causes of the women profiled range from gracious entertaining to women's suffrage. In Lulie's case, Luckett didn't have much to say other than to mention her missionary work and the college.

It is census records and Lulie's obituary that lend a little dimension to her story. By 1950, Lulie was living with her partner Gertrude Nickerson in an apartment building on 100 West University Parkway. Gertrude was also a Goucher graduate, from the class of 1899. When Hooper died in 1955, she left $5000 (today's equivalent of roughly 60,000) in a trust to Nickerson.

Society pages through the years mentioned Lulie, Gertrude, or both, in snippets that suggest a life of traveling and socializing with intellectuals, many of them Goucher alumni. Although I found no indication of suffrage activism on either of their parts, they would have interacted with Baltimore suffragettes, philanthropists, and patrons of the arts.

When Gertrude died in 1964, she was not buried at Green Mount with her partner, but in Pennsylvania with her parents.

Outside of some items that Lulie Hooper donated to Goucher College's art collection, her contribution to the artistic and intellectual life of Baltimore in the early 19th century is largely undocumented. Thanks to her three additions to the Lovely Lane Cookbook —for Mint Sauce, Imperial Cake, and this salad dressing— we at least get a glimpse into her culinary world.

HARVEY SALAD DRESSING

1 pint olive oil
2 Sterno beef tablets
20 chopped olives
¼ pound Roquefort cheese chopped
2 buttons garlic chopped
1 teaspoon paprika
1 tablespoon salt

½ pint apple vinegar
2 tablespoons sugar
2 tablespoons capers
½ pint tomato catsup
2 tablespoons Worcestershire sauce
cayenne pepper to taste

This will make a quart of dressing which will keep until used.

recipe from "Lovely Lane Cook Book," The Woman's Guild, First Methodist Episcopal Church, 1936

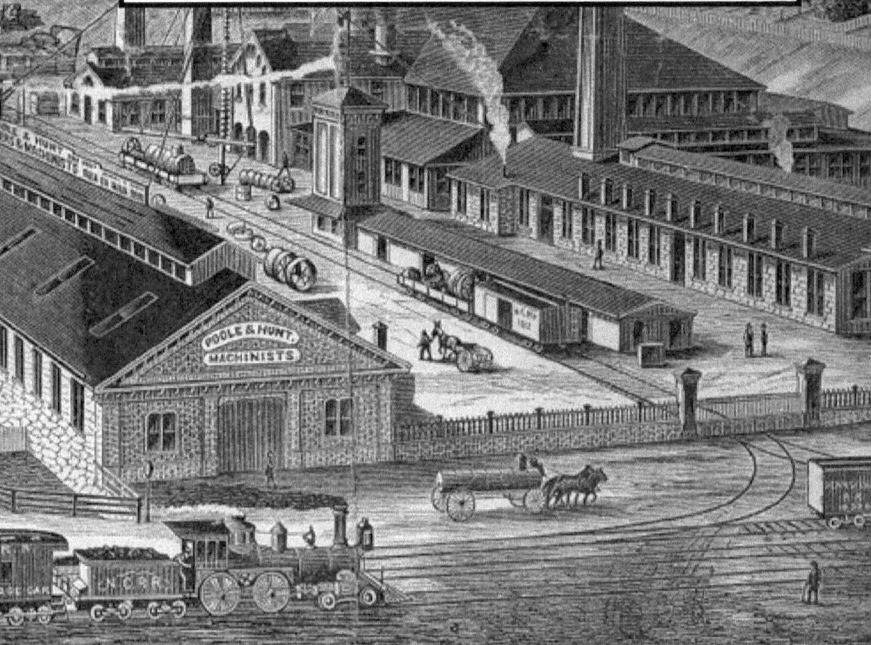

FOUNDRY AND MACHINE WORKS OF POOLE & HU

BALTIMORE, MD.

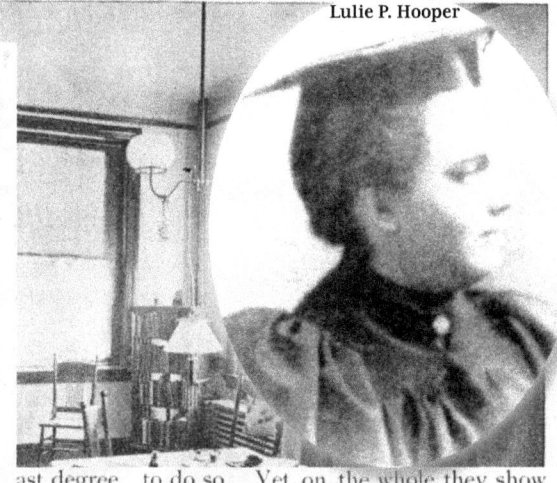

Lulie P. Hooper

MISS HOOPER RITES TODAY

Goucher Trustee Long Active In Missionary Work

Miss Lulie Poole Hooper, a member of the board of trustees of Goucher College and long active in Methodist Church missionary affairs, died yesterday at Union Memorial Hospital following a brief illness. She was 80.

Miss Hooper was the granddaughter of the late William E. Hooper, founder of the Hooper Mills at Woodberry.

Shortly after her graduation from Goucher in the class of 1896, of which she was president, she became a member of the Foreign Missionary Society of the Methodist Church.

Miss Hooper, following many missionary trips through the Pacific and the Orient, gave numerous pieces of art to Goucher. The college showed its love and respect for her by naming Hooper Hall in her honor.

Funeral services will be held at the Lovely Lane Methodist Church, of which she was a member, at 2 P.M. today. The Rev. Kenneth R. Ross will officiate. Burial will be in Greenmount Cemetery.

e ... ast degree
s ... akness or
d ... gned with
t ... machines,

to do so. Yet on the whole they show no little zest for it. In the spring, when the exercises that have been carried on since September begin to grow some-

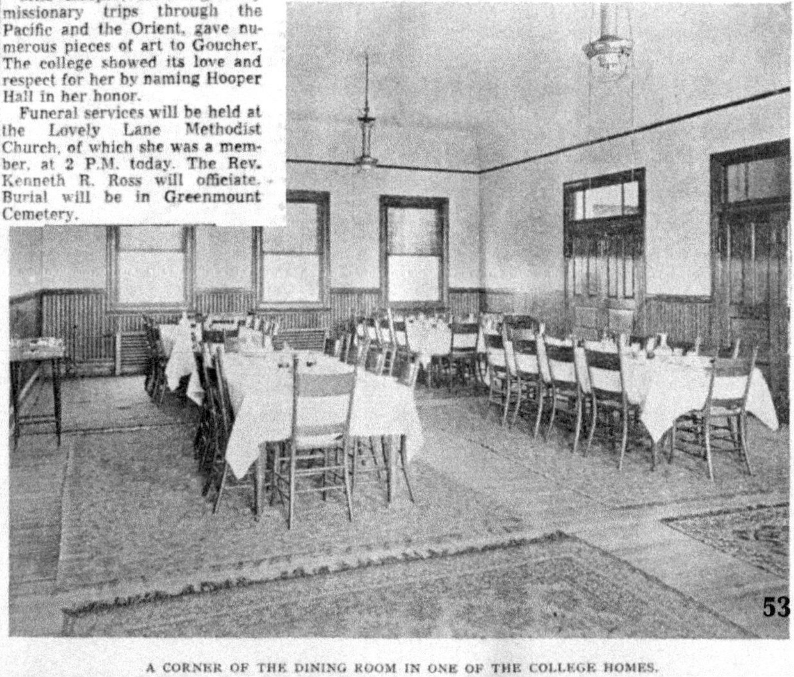

A CORNER OF THE DINING ROOM IN ONE OF THE COLLEGE HOMES.

❧Mulligatawny Soup❧

H. J. McGrath
1843-1909
Daisy Area, plot 65

Thanks to free repositories like the Internet Archive, we can now browse hundreds of old trade publications that chronicle Baltimore's industrial past. Newsletters like "Canning Age," "The Canning Trade," "The Canned Goods Trade," and "Canner and Dried Fruit Packer" may not have had the most creative or catchy names, but their insides are full of business listings, contemporary news, and illustrated advertisements of equipment for the processing, packing, and labeling of food.

The February 1909 issue of "The Canned Goods Trade" reported on the death of Mr. Henry J. McGrath, "president of the H. J. McGrath Company, one of the oldest oyster packing establishments in Baltimore." Opposite McGrath's obituary is a full-page ad, unrelated, for Bolgiano's "Greater Baltimore Tomato," purported to be the best tomato for packers for 91 years. A search for the word "Baltimore" turns up 127 results in the 38-page publication. When it came to canning, Baltimore was a big deal.

H. J. McGrath was a big deal too. In addition to his canning business, he was the president of a bank, Canton National Bank of Baltimore. He was also regularly called upon by trade publications to report on prices for produce such as peas, carrots and tomatoes— in effect setting industry standard.

McGrath was born in Pocomoke City in 1843. According to a biography in a souvenir booklet for the 1904 World's Fair, he "followed the sea four years" as a youth before entering the canning business. In addition to the bank, he was president of the Canned Goods Exchange, the Boys' Home, and was on the Jail Board. "Mr. McGrath is married, and has a beautiful home at 1023 St. Paul Street."

Perhaps par for the course for a large business, the McGrath name is also associated with a number of lawsuits as plaintiff and defendant, for breach of contract, shipping damaged items, having items damaged by the railroad during shipping, libel, and disputes over deliveries of crops.

Not all of these documents involve McGrath directly, as his eponymous

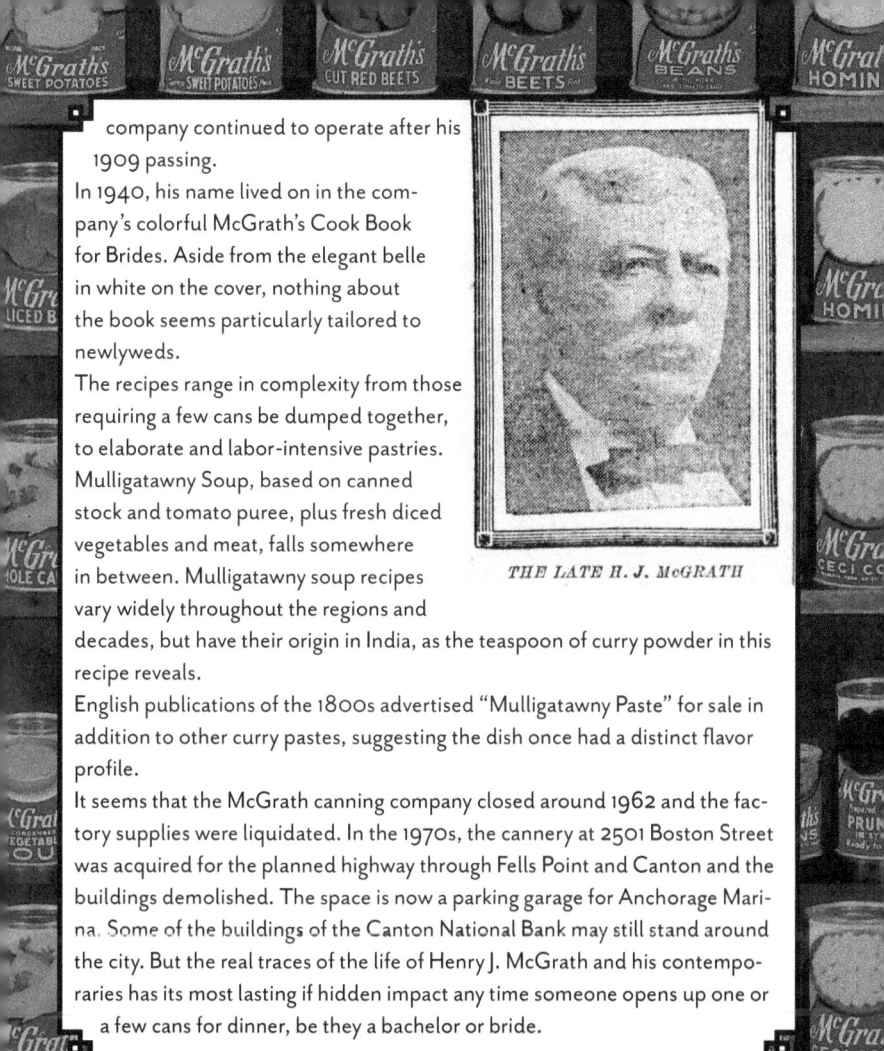

company continued to operate after his 1909 passing.

In 1940, his name lived on in the company's colorful McGrath's Cook Book for Brides. Aside from the elegant belle in white on the cover, nothing about the book seems particularly tailored to newlyweds.

The recipes range in complexity from those requiring a few cans be dumped together, to elaborate and labor-intensive pastries. Mulligatawny Soup, based on canned stock and tomato puree, plus fresh diced vegetables and meat, falls somewhere in between. Mulligatawny soup recipes vary widely throughout the regions and decades, but have their origin in India, as the teaspoon of curry powder in this recipe reveals.

THE LATE H. J. McGRATH

English publications of the 1800s advertised "Mulligatawny Paste" for sale in addition to other curry pastes, suggesting the dish once had a distinct flavor profile.

It seems that the McGrath canning company closed around 1962 and the factory supplies were liquidated. In the 1970s, the cannery at 2501 Boston Street was acquired for the planned highway through Fells Point and Canton and the buildings demolished. The space is now a parking garage for Anchorage Marina. Some of the buildings of the Canton National Bank may still stand around the city. But the real traces of the life of Henry J. McGrath and his contemporaries has its most lasting if hidden impact any time someone opens up one or a few cans for dinner, be they a bachelor or bride.

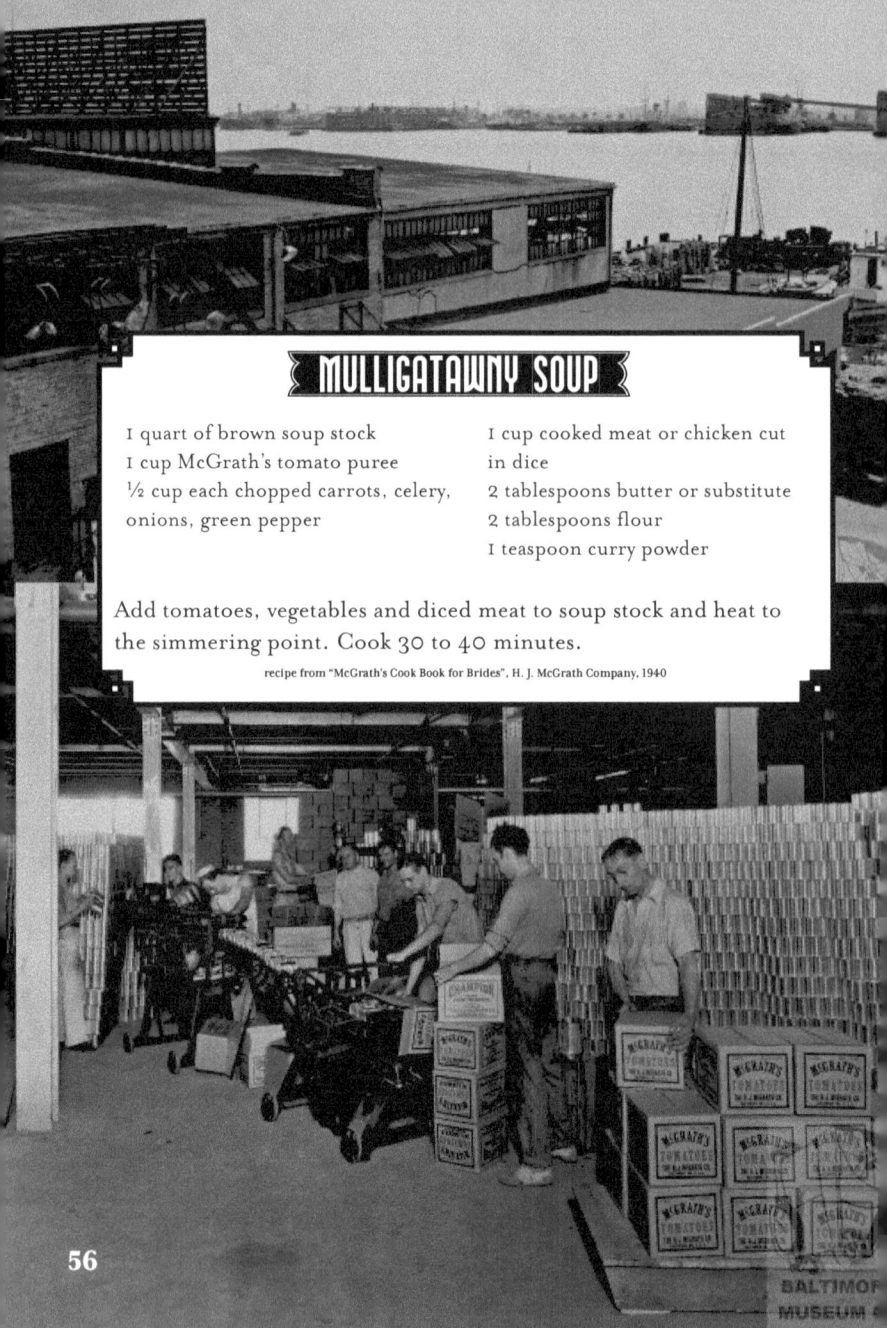

MULLIGATAWNY SOUP

1 quart of brown soup stock
1 cup McGrath's tomato puree
½ cup each chopped carrots, celery, onions, green pepper

1 cup cooked meat or chicken cut in dice
2 tablespoons butter or substitute
2 tablespoons flour
1 teaspoon curry powder

Add tomatoes, vegetables and diced meat to soup stock and heat to the simmering point. Cook 30 to 40 minutes.

recipe from "McGrath's Cook Book for Brides", H. J. McGrath Company, 1940

McGrath's
COOK BOOK
for BRIDES

❦ Jumbles ❧

Elizabeth Bose Marye
1853-1928
Section I, plot 111

The collections left to the Maryland Center for History and Culture (formerly the Maryland Historical Society) by William Bose Marye are extensive: family photographs, savings account books, schoolwork, genealogies, correspondence, and much of Marye's own research material.

Among the papers is a handwritten manuscript cookbook, probably compiled by Marye's mother, Elizabeth Mary Bose Marye. Mrs. Marye recorded the usual. There are baked goods like Sally Lunn Bread, raisin loaf, Ginger Bread, and fruit cake. She saved a recipe for "Robert E. Lee Cake," a jelly-filled layer cake that is often an indicator of political alignment (but not always - it is a cake.) Marye collected beverage recipes for Egg Nogg, drinking chocolate and the potent Cherry Bounce. She saved remedies for dysentery, sore throat, and a "valuable hair tonic." Her recipe for Jumbles, a type of sugar cookie often shaped into a ring, is characteristically sparse for the 19th century. It doesn't even tell you how to bake them.

One recipe is attributed to "Miss Eliza Ellicott." On first glance, I would expect

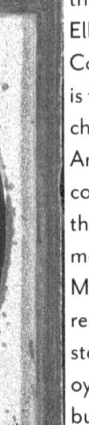

Arabella Young Gittings, Elizabeth Mary Bose Gittings' mother

this to be copied from Elizabeth Ellicott Lea's 1845 book "Domestic Cookery," except that the recipe is for caramels - somewhat out of character for the Quaker author. And indeed, "Domestic Cookery" contains no recipe for caramels— this recipe came from another member of the Ellicott family. Marye's recipe for oyster soup resembles most Maryland "oyster stew" or "stewed oyster" recipes - oysters in a thickened milk broth, but she included marjoram and thyme, a nice addition to the usual black pepper.

Born in 1886 in Baltimore County, William Bose Marye was a historian and amateur archaeologist who documented Maryland's Native American sites. Each year, the Archaeological Society of Maryland awards a "William B. Marye Award" to honor "individuals who have made outstanding contributions to Maryland archeology." Marye had a love of Maryland and Maryland history, but his parents originally hailed from Fredericksburg Virginia, where there is a historical marker noting "Marye's Battery." "This battery fired the first cannon of the battle," it states, "... opened at intervals upon the Union lines..." Oh. Well, maybe Elizabeth didn't just love jelly cake after all.

William Bose Marye wrote poetry in addition to his historical pursuits. A poem entitled "On Walking In A Cornfield In August" makes reference to his archaeological work:

"O cornfield of midsummer, seldom visited; I went to you for the mysterious arrowhead. Hour after hour, between the corn rows, in the sun; I trudged your aisles, contented if I found but one."

The lineage Marye so carefully traced ended with him. He never married and left no children. But the many books he wrote and the huge collection he left behind will mean he's remembered by generations of historians to come.

FAREWELL TO MARYLAND

The helpless landscape dies
Of brutal hands laid on it
By greedy men that scorn it.
'Tis murdered where it lies.

On stricken earth and sward—
Fields, meadows, woods and
beaches,
The tidal river's reaches—
They turn the urban horde.

When naught remains to bless,
Ye who have loved this land,
Make heard your reprimand:
   A curse on their success.

JUMBLES

1 Lb brown sugar

1 Lb butter

1 ½ Lb flour

1 nutmeg

3 eggs

recipe from the William Bose Marye collection,
MS 2458. H. Furlong Baldwin Library.

ᏒRabbit "German Style" Ꮢ

Matilda Backus Maloy
1880-1964
Section EE, plot 4

"Maryland women will vote in 1920," Matilda Maloy told the Women's Club. It was November 4, 1919, a year from the election. "The fight for suffrage is practically at an end." That past May, the Nineteenth Amendment had passed. By the end of that year, twenty-two states ratified the amendment. Maryland was not one of them.

Despite the ardent work by Maryland suffragettes, the state did not veer towards giving women the vote. While many states in the west had granted women full suffrage, and others allowed women to vote in municipal, presidential, or school and tax elections, a band of states from Pennsylvania to Alabama granted women little to no electoral powers.

It was not for a lack of activism. As early as 1648, landowner Margaret Brent had stood before Maryland legislature and requested her right to vote. Two centuries later, Maryland women were slowly gaining traction in the fight for equal representation.

Matilda Backus Maloy was among those women. As publicity chair for the Woman Suffrage League of Maryland, Maloy urged suffrage groups from all of the counties of Maryland to report their activities for publication. "The only way for the full value of the work of the Women's Section... to be recognized by the general public is through publicity."

During World War I, Maloy had been appointed by Governor Emerson Harrington to be secretary of the Women's Section for the Maryland Council of Defense. Activities included serving on a home economics committee to teach homemakers safe preservation techniques under the direction of the Maryland Agricultural College, and securing volunteers to tabulate censuses for the draft.

In 1913, Matilda wed state senator William Milnes Maloy. She remained heavily involved in his career - and in politics and volunteering in general, throughout her life. She promoted causes like directing state and federal funding towards studies to prevent maternal and infant mortality. During World War II, she worked thousands of hours volunteering for the Red Cross. Her war and family-oriented activities tied in with her commitment to the suffrage cause.

In a 1919 letter to the Baltimore Sun in response to Mrs. M. J. Zollinger, secretary of the Maryland Association Opposed to Woman Suffrage, Maloy wrote "the Anti-Suffragists rest their cause on the plea that the family must be preserved and that this demands the self-effacement of all individuality and the complete surrender of every right by the human beings composing the family...Those who advocate woman suffrage believe: '1. That women who pay taxes should, on equal terms with men, vote for those who make the laws relating to the distribution of those taxes for the public good. 2. That women, who obey the laws, should help to choose those who make the laws. 3. That laws which affect children should embody the woman's point of view as well as the man's....7... the nearly 12,000,000 women wage-earners in the United States should be permitted a voice in the making of the laws which govern the conditions under which they labor. 9. That the ballot is the ultimate source of power in a democracy.. And since the United States claims to be a democracy.. Women for no other reason than that they are women, cannot consistently be denied the right to vote.'"

Cookbooks and recipes were tools in the arsenal of suffragettes. While some groups simply raised money by compiling cookbooks, Hattie A. Burr of Massachusetts shared her recipes for Brown Bread, Quince Preserve, household hints and more followed by pages of "Eminent Opinions on Woman Suffrage" from Abraham Lincoln, Henry Wadsworth Longfellow, John Stuart Mill, Harriet Beecher Stowe, Louisa May Alcott, and a host of other well-respected thinkers. Burr entitled her 1890 book "The Woman suffrage cook book," and it was one of many suffrage-themed cookbooks of the

MRS. WILLIAM MILNES MALOY

Efficiency Written Large

time. In addition to raising money and spreading ideas, the books may have served as a reassurance that suffrage wouldn't presage an abandonment of domestic duties.

In Western Maryland, The Oakland Civic Club capitalized on the state's culinary renown with the 1914 "Maryland Cook Book." The Civic Club was founded with the mission of "cleaning up the streets" of downtown Oakland, but the cookbook contains recipes from Dr. Lorilla Bullard Tower, a prominent Western Maryland feminist. One can imagine club meetings were a space for discussion if not organizing.

The 1926 "Recipe Book" produced by the Alumnæ association of Eastern Female High School was not a suffrage cookbook, but the education of young women aligned with the suffrage movement.

For her lone contribution to the Recipe Book, Matilda chose a heritage recipe for Hasenpfeffer, which she simply called "Rabbit (German Style)." Her gravy is thickened with gingersnaps, which is not unheard of, but is more common to Sauerbraten, a beef version popularly known as "Sour Beef" in Baltimore. The sweet and tangy combination of vinegar, cookies, and pickling spices is an acquired taste, but for a lot of Baltimoreans it is comfort-food.

Maloy's parents, Justus Backus and Christina Fredericka emigrated from Germany before Matilda's birth in 1880. Like many German Baltimoreans, Justus was a laborer. According to the 1880 census he worked at an iron foundry. Matilda was very involved with her husband's campaigns and senatorial and Public Services Commission careers. She earned a political science degree at Johns Hopkins.

Matilda's husband William's career in politics was long. He made a play for the Maryland governorship in 1926. Despite —or perhaps because of— an endorsement from the Anti-Saloon League of Maryland, Maloy lost the Democratic nomination to incumbent Albert Ritchie, who he'd had a long-running political feud with.

Disappointingly, Matilda Maloy demonstrated the racist politics that sully the legacy of so many white suffragettes. When Southern states worried that universal suffrage would empower Black people, Maloy wrote that "anti-suffragists will tell you that negroes will rule the South when women vote... That race will continue superior which is superior and the talk of 'negro domination' is a bug-a-boo which will frighten no man when he knows the facts."

In actuality, Black women contributed a great deal to the cause for women's suffrage. Marylanders like poet Frances Ellen Watkins Harper and missionary Mary Frisby Handy led and organized movements despite being excluded from events organized by whites.

Interestingly, William, on the other hand, had his own obituary in the Afro-American when he died in 1949. He had been a teacher at the "Colored Polytechnic Institute," earned the nickname of "Irish Pat," and, according to the obituary, "to him color was not important."

Maryland ratified the Nineteenth Amendment in 1941. By then, it was only a symbolic gesture. Legislature waited until 1958 to certify the vote.

Throughout her life until her 1964 death, for better or worse, Matilda Maloy was involved in politics, volunteering, and public life. It seems she sought to embody the ideal she espoused in 1920, when she wrote to the Westminster Democratic Advocate: "What is the matter with the Southern women, including those of Maryland, that they should be excluded [from voting]?.. The South will find...but one answer to the question. There is nothing the matter with Southern women. Their political acumen, their wit, their beauty, their enthusiasm, enliven and strengthen every gathering in the land."

RABBIT GERMAN STYLE

Clean rabbit thoroughly, cut into pieces as for frying, rinse well. Place in earthen bowl, sprinkle with salt and cover fully with equal portions of water and vinegar. Let stand for several hours. Put rabbit and liquid in agate or aluminum pot and add to it 1 tablespoon of mixed allspice and cloves with 3 or 4 bay leaves. (The spices may be tied in a little cheese-cloth bag and suspended or placed in the liquid to prevent the necessity of picking them out afterwards.) Let the rabbit simmer in the liquid with the spices until tender. Skim occasionally. If too acid to suit taste, add a little sugar. When done, remove the bag from the spices and thicken with a mixture of flour, 6 or 7 old-fashioned ginger cookies and cold water. Serve with boiled or mashed white potatoes. (For more than one rabbit increase proportions accordingly.)

recipe from Recipe Book, Alumnæ Eastern Female High School, 1926.

Crab Imperial

Honolulu McKeldin
1900-1988
Cedar Area, plot 14

Whether it was first served at Thompson's Sea Girt House (as the story goes) or elsewhere, Crab Imperial came onto the scene at just the right time. Decadent and creamy recipes like Chicken A La King and Lobster Newburg were also reaching ubiquity in fashionable hotels, railroad cars, clubs and homes. These dishes were often served up in a vessel that was the height of Gilded Age presentation: the chafing dish. Before stove-top pressure cookers, George Foreman Grills, or air fryers dominated counter space in American kitchens, the chafing dish became the necessary accessory for fashionable entertaining. Famously used for dorm-room or "bachelor" cooking, a slew of cookbooks with tailor-made recipes were published to meet demand. Most contained the same few dishes.

In fine dining settings, the chafing dish was used to serve food at the table, not to cook it. One writer took issue with this. In a little expose in the Kansas City Weekly News in 1906, the chafing dish was declared a "bluff." "The stuff that's served in them is not cooked in a chafing dish either before or after it reaches the table," the writer indignantly pointed out.

And so the chafing dish as a cookery fad died out. The dishes that rose alongside it persisted.

Crab Imperial, a.k.a. Imperial Crab, was Honolulu McKeldin's go-to recipe when community organizations reached out to her for a cookbook contribution, and I have her recipe in the 1958 edition of "Recipes Old and New," compiled by the St. Anne's Parish in Annapolis, as well as "The Women of St. Barnabas Church Oxon Hill Cookbook" from 1954.

The St. Anne's recipe appears to have some typos. Ingredients that were called for in tablespoons in 1954 are called for in teaspoons, and some measurements are confusingly omitted. To look at the recipe you would never know. You would just be disappointed in the result.

It's a shame that Mrs. McKeldin's Crab Imperial would get botched in this way, because that recipe is one of the few things that frames her in the spotlight. When I went to research her, I was surprised at the relative dearth of information and profiles I came across compared to say, Helen Tawes, another Maryland first lady associated with food. Honolulu McKeldin said she preferred to tend to her home life instead of getting involved in politics like her husband Theodore, who served as Mayor of Baltimore and later, Governor. He was known for championing Civil Rights and going against the Republican party because of his beliefs. In 1967, city hall reporter Robert Loevy said of Theodore McKeldin, "He has minority appeal. He puts together a weird combination of poor Negroes and wealthy whites." Whether taken as criticism or compliment, he wasn't the last politician to be described thusly.

Later in life, Honolulu lived in Baltimore's Homeland neighborhood and volunteered at Union Memorial Hospital. She gave an interview to the Evening Sun in 1978 in which she regretted how hard she had worked in the Governor's mansion, striving to run a household with as little hired help as possible. Her husband had died four years earlier in 1974. If she were to do it over, she said "I would have had a housekeeper. I would have worked less, and I probably would have enjoyed it more. I took it too seriously." Still, at that time she sat with her "extremely well-behaved white toy poodle" Sugar and was content with doing her own cooking and cleaning and gardening.

Again, this was little detail and color for the wife of a man so controversially embroiled in desegregation in a state with Southern sensibilities. Even if she just enabled his nonstop campaigning by keeping the mansion in order, she was a part of it all. "By the time I got finished, I felt I should have had a salary," she told the Sun.

Mrs. 'Mac' Will Be Popul

State's 'First Lady' in Her Favorite Pose

As to Honolulu's odd name, the article said "her mother, having named several children before her, was at a loss for another name... so she turned to her doctor and asked 'What shall I call her? The doctor said 'I have no idea, but I've always wanted to go to Honolulu. Why don't you name her Honolulu?'" Even the story of her name is anticlimactic. But I suspect there was much more to Honolulu McKeldin than we will ever know.

(Continued

spoils them. And
a better husban
he is getting nov
"He has work
Christian life.
certain he puts
all else. Most pe
how religious he
"Only circums
enter the law in
school of theolo
preach, and does
gets the chance.
"Sometimes I wonder whether
he does not walk he had gone into
the ministry."

Leaves Politics to Him

About her role in politics, the
First Lady said, "I acquaint myself with a few facts and leave the
politicking in the family to Mr.
McKeldin."

Then suddenly changing the subject, she said, "I know you have
been wondering about all the
statuettes and figurines around
this room (I had been, there are
dozens of them). Well, the people
belong to Mr. McKeldin, and I
gave him three more for Christmas.

"The China dogs belong to Clara
(she's the McKeldins' 10-year-old
daughter). She also collects dolls
and has quite a few. They are all

ways as personal friends.
"You know," she revealed, "Mr.
Callaway comes here so often he
is like one of the family." She ex-
plained further, "I feel about people according to the way they
meet me. I don't see anyone as
colored, but as a person. If I like
someone, I consider that person as
a friend.
"I feel every one of the ladies
who sent me the prayerbook is a
friend, not just an acquaintance."
Mrs. McKeldin likes tailored
clothes, boasts more suits in her
wardrobe than anything else, but
says she will dress up when the
occasion demands.
She serves on the boards of the
Three Arts Club, which has a
membership of 350; the Homeland
Garden Club, the Women's Civic
League and the Empty Stocking

Mrs. McKeldin See: An Easier Pace For Pat Hughes

By Josephine Novak

Faced with constant rounds of entertaining, life is never easy for a governor's wife. But Honolulu McKeldin, wid-
ow of former Gov. Theodore R. McKeldin (1951-1959), thinks the machinery
exists today to give the First Lady of
Maryland a somewhat easier life than
she experienced in Annapolis.

Asked what Patricia Hughes will encounter when her husband, Harry, takes
office in January, Mrs. McKeldin said,
"In many ways, it was different for me
than it would be now.

"Things have changed so much. For
one thing, we didn't have all the security
Government House has today. If we
were there in the evenings, we liked to
let the help go off the floor at 9 p.m. Often, at night, Ted used to answer the tel-
ephone himself and, before retiring,
would run around to see that all the
doors were locked.

"Once, when I looked down from the
second floor, I saw a person I had never
seen before walking through the down-
stairs rooms. I was really frightened."

Smiling warmly, with an easy charm,
Mrs. McKeldin relaxed in the living
room of her house in Homeland. Wearing a tailored, blue wool dress and jack-

I worked too hard. And all those s
groups and other groups to be s
through—it kept me awfully busy
the time I got finished, I felt I s
have had a salary."

Mrs. McKeldin said the help a
mansion was not well paid wher
was there, and that the cook prep
only plain Southern cooking—"s
times it turned out well and some
it didn't." Big parties had to be ca
because the cook couldn't handle th

"We bought quite a few art of
for the house and some furniture.
of the furniture in the living quart
the house had been—how shall I s
—ordinary. There were an awful
linens to be replaced, too. I had so
teas. Looking back on it, it seemed
ybody wanted a tea. The house
have any particularly nice linen, s
all Quaker cloth sewn together, s
bought some new linen.

"Eisenhower was in office wh
were in Annapolis. Many of his a
would visit the Naval Academy an

66

THE McKELDINS AT HOME—Marse-cheif Theodore R. McKeldin with daughter Clara, receives congratulations.   ALL SMILES, Mr. McKeldin, with Mrs. McKeldin and Clara, sits for a photographer in congratulatory banquet.   in the living room of the family home at 332 St. Dunstans road, in suburban Homeland.   OFF TO SCHOOL—It was just another school day for son Tevis, 8, a student at Gilman School.

McKeldin
Mayoralty

Elkton

CRAB IMPERIAL

1 lb. crab meat	1 egg (raw)
1 hard boiled egg, minced to a paste	1 - ½ cup stale bread crumbs, fine
1 - ½ Tbsp. minced pimentos	1 - ½ Tbsp. of minced green peppers
1 Tbsp. minced parsley	par boiled until tender
2 Tbsp. Worcestershire sauce	Salt and pepper
2 Tbsp. mayonnaise	1 Tbsp. melted butter

Mix all together and put in clean [crab] shells. Makes 4 - top with thinned mayonnaise. Cook in a 350° F. oven for 15 minutes or until a light brown.

recipe from "The Women of St. Barnabas Church Oxon Hill Cookbook," The Women of St. Barnabas Church. 1954.

Dear Mrs. Mee:

    This will acknowledge your letter of December 12th, and enclosures.

    In accord with your request, it was a great pleasure for me to autograph the recipe for Imperial Crab, and it is returned herewith.

    With kindest regards, and best wishes for a joyous holiday season, I am,

Sincerely,

Mrs. Theodore R. McKeldin.

Mrs. Mary L. Mee
Box 95
Kennedy, New York.

A Gallery Of Governors' Wive

HONORED: McKELDIN
Wife of former Governor Theodore R. McKeldin

67

Russian Borscht

Allen Welsh Dulles
1893-1969
McDonough Area, plot 52

You might not know that the "world's largest accessible private collection of government documents and public records relating to the assassination of President John F. Kennedy" is kept at Hood College in Frederick. I certainly didn't, until I made a chicken recipe by Harold Weisberg. It turned out that the Frederick-area man, also a chicken farmer, tasked himself with taking down the perceived incompetence of the Warren Commission. He wrote seven books about it.

Weisberg's obsession was a little over the top, but he was far from the only person with questions. And when they go seeking answers, they are bound to come across Allen Dulles.

Born in Watertown New York, Dulles came from a family of high-ranking government officials. His brother John Foster Dulles, for whom the airport is named, was Secretary of State. Allen served in the Office of Strategic Services before making his way into Central Intelligence, where he eventually became Director.

Dulles' controversies are many, even outside of his bungling of the Bay of Pigs, subsequent dismissal by John F. Kennedy, and possible involvement in the assassination.

Dulles' fixation with and loathing of Soviet Russia was boundless, and his ethos was that there are no rules in war. Feeling constricted by lack of access to "human guinea pigs" to experiment on, he authorized the MKUltra program in hopes that LSD could be used for mind control to create super-assassins. This led to the demise of a Maryland man, Frank Olson, a biochemist at Fort Detrick, who was dosed with acid and (allegedly) killed himself by crashing out a tenth-story window in Manhattan.

Dulles' preoccupation with taking down Communism ran so deep that he felt it would be advisable to rehabilitate some Nazi leaders. "Most men of the caliber [required to run Germany] suffer a political taint," he once said.

He worked behind the scenes to shorten the sentences of some of those

convicted in the Nuremberg Trials.

Another bizarre episode is described in Stephen Kinzer's "The Brothers: John Foster Dulles, Allen Dulles, and Their Secret World War." In an attempt to take down Sukarno, President of Indonesia, Allen commissioned a pornographic movie called "Happy Days," featuring an actor wearing a Sukarno mask. The CIA distributed prints of the film around East Asia to humiliate their rival, to little effect. "Far more potent were the tons of weaponry that poured onto docks and spilled from the sky in rebel-held Indonesia, courtesy of the CIA," wrote Kinzer. You don't say.

In 1920, well before his ascent to becoming the "Master of Spies," Dulles met Martha Clover Todd. He proposed within a week. Clover Todd Dulles' mother hailed from a wealthy Baltimore family by the name of Gilman (distant relations of Johns Hopkins President Daniel Coit Gilman.) In letters held at the Maryland Center for History and Culture, Clover's family call her "Clo-Clo." Clover Dulles is sometimes described as having been a feisty flapper, but she did not fight her way out of a marriage that entailed, according to Allen's own sister "more than a hundred affairs" including a longtime relationship with novelist and spy Mary Bancroft. Clover is said to have condoned the affair. According to Dulles biography "The Devil's Chessboard," "this story gives Clover an authority over Allen's amorous adventures that, in reality, she sorely lacked."

"The Devil's Chessboard" was the most sensational and compelling of the Dulles biographies I referenced, but the basic facts of his life and career are corroborated in James Srodes' "Allen Dulles Master of Spies," a more sympathetic biography that contained a lot of weird commentary, including the following, referring to the Dulles family during Allen's childhood: "There was a robust sexuality that ran through most of their lives." That book makes the case that Dulles' actions (such as drugging people) were reasonable responses to the threat of Communism.

When I found out that Allen Dulles was buried at Green Mount Cemetery, I wondered if I could find a recipe associated with him. I did research into his wife Clover, and then his mother, Edith. I found Edith mentioned in conjunction with the Auburn New York Woman's Union. "I wonder if they ever made a cookbook?" Bingo.

I had Harvard Library scan the book and I eagerly awaited the files.

Memorandum

FROM

SUBJECT:

When I received them, there were two recipes. A "Luncheon Dish" featuring vegetables in a cream sauce, and "Russian Borscht." This is an amusing coincidence but is probably due to the fact that Edith's father John W. Foster was the United States Minister to Russia from 1880-1881.

Edith was described in "The Brothers" as "one of the most cosmopolitan young American women of her generation." Her father, who promoted corporate interests in Washington after his retirement from the government, was a huge influence on Allen and his brother John.

Due to Martha Clover Todd's deep connections to Baltimore, Allen Dulles lies at Green Mount along with so much Baltimore history. Some have pointed out the irony of his sharing a resting place with John Wilkes Booth. By the time of his 1969 death, newspapers covered the life of Allen Dulles with a bit of curiosity and perhaps irreverence. His obituary in the Baltimore Sun, which mentions his burial at Green Mount, ended with a quote from TASS, the official Soviet News agency: "[Mr. Dulles] fiercely hated the Soviet Union."

of CIA
occurre
to be
whether
agencie
believe

CIA?"
any evi
Kennedy?
question will be "What suggestions does CIA have to offer for
guarding
didn't
nature
already
Soviet
reflec
cannot

⟩ RUSSIAN BORSCH SOUP ⟨

Shank beef, about 3lbs. Cook slowly all day. Strain and leave over night. In morning skim off all fat. Cook three large or six small beets. Heat stock and grate beets into it.

When serving, put on top, one teaspoon of sour cream.

recipe from "The Woman's Union Cook Book," The Women's Educational and Industrial Union, 1932

that C
with t
these do
relations with such a person as Oswald. However, on the other
CIA has no evidence that Oswald was under the instructions of
directorate charged with assassinations.

said if anything further developed today which
be helpful to us, he would call.

REC-11   105-82555

RECOMMENDATION:

For the information of the Director.   b?G-FBI   2 MAY 14 19

WCS:1m1/ (7)
1 - Mr. Belmont
1 - Mr. Sullivan
1 - D. E. Moore
1 - Mr. J.A.Sizoo
1 - Mr. Branigan

2 2 NOV 1974   Dulles, Alle

Allen Dulles Testified CIA, FB

By Donald P. Baker
Washington Post Staff Writer

Newly declassified documents reveal that former

dent anything, commission member John J. McCloy, asked Dulles: "You wouldn't tell the Secretary of Defense?"

"Well, it depends a little bit on the circumstances."

ployee of the bureau in any capacity, either as an agent or as a special employee, or as an informant."

CIA director McCone testified the same day as Hoo-

Wels
ic of
said
'alled
the
had

Would Li

Garrison subpoenas ex-CIA head

LA Free Press 3/6/8 K

STEVEN

NEW O

The Distri
cumann
ok Alle
the
one
lles
nml

purchase several trucks from the
Bolton Ford Company for the
Friends of Democratic Cuba.
Oscar Deslatte, assistant man-

TIME
THE WEEKLY NEWSMAGAZINE

CENTRAL INTELLIGENCE AGENCY ALLEN DULLES

r/JFKresearcher · 1 yr. ago
walterherbst

Allen Dulles Buried Near John Wilkes Booth Hidden Message?

UNITED STATES

FEDERAL INTELLIGENCE AGENCY
BROAD STREET N.W.
WASHINGTON D.C.
Is to Certify that

Allen W. Dulles

Mrs. ALLEN DULLES.

do/-2 airfield. Among all of Oswald's friends and acquaintances mentioned in the Warren Report, there appears no left-wingers or communists but many rightists.

Dulles ended his tenure as Director of the CIA in 1961 while Oswald was in the Sovie

reported that Garris
New Orleans on Januar
Jan, which two men, one
rsed the name Oswald

Subpoena
Is Issued
For Dulle

NEW ORLEANS, March
(UPI)—A judge today orden
former Central Intellige
Agency Director Allen Dul
to answer a subpoena in N
Orleans March 28 and 29
District Attorney Jim Ga
son's investigation of the K
nedy assassination.

District Judge Matth
Braniff signed the ord
which would grant Dulles f
munity from prosecution, a
instructed it be sent to 1
home in Washington.

Garrison subpoensed Dull

-Chief of CIA
llen W. Dulles
Dead at 75

SF 1/30/69

HINGTON (AP)—Allen
les, America's master
steered the Central
ence Agency through
ars of controversial in-
nal intrigue, died late
ay. He was 75.
s, appointed CIA chief
by former President
D. Eisenhower, retired
ate life in 1961 follow-
Bay of Pigs invasion
—which, with an ear-

ed Green Mount Cemetery in Baltimore, Maryland, to see the grav
incoln's assassin, John Wilkes Booth. It is a tiny headstone withou
m in the attached photo, and very difficult to find. If you look clos
nnies lying near the he
with Lincoln's image lo
later, people still hono

Mount, I was surprise
as also buried there. I v
n Washington D.C. or ir
y connection he had to

I called Green Mount t
Martha "Clover" Todd
a simple explanation. M

World War, Cold War and the House of Dulles

DULLES: A biography of Eleanor, Allen and John Foster Dulles and Their Family Network.
Both Leonard Mosley. Dial Press.
$12.95

By DANIEL VERGIN

71

Works Cited

Correspondence, 1824 - 1835, Box: 1, Folder: 1. Benjamin Chew Howard manuscript collection, MS 3159. H. Furlong Baldwin Library.

Davis, Harry Alexander, b. 1875.The Junkins Family: Descendants of Robert Junkins of York County, Maine. Washington DC: [Mimeoform service],1938.

Forrest, Clarence H.Beacon Lights of Baltimore: A Souvenir of the Louisiana Purchase Exposition Or World's Fair, Held In St. Louis, Missouri, May 1 to November 30, 1904.Baltimore: Press of Summers Printing Co,1904.

Johnson, Gerald White, and Pleasants, Jacob Hall. Green Mount Cemetery One Hundredth Anniversary, 1838-1938. United States, Green Mount Cemetery, 1938.

Luckett, Margie Hersh. Maryland Women: Baltimore, Maryland, 1931-1942.Baltimore: King Bros., Press,19311942.

Mabel Roberts cookbook, n.d., MS 2755, H. Furlong Baldwin Library, Maryland Center for History and Culture, Baltimore.

Maryland in the World War 1917-1919; Military and Naval Service Records, Volumes I & II

Series IV: Extended Family Papers, circa 1876-1904, undated, Box: 1, Folder: 9. Marye-Gittings collection, MS 0563. H. Furlong Baldwin Library.

Stapleton & Co's Topographical History and Directory. United Kingdom, Stapleton&Company, 1838.

The Records of the Wine and Food Society of Baltimore, Special Collections, Enoch Pratt Free Library/ Maryland's State Library Resource Center.

"6520. Misbranding of Canned Peas and Canned Tomatoes. U. S. V. The H. J. McGrath Co. Plea of Guilty. Fine, $125 and Costs. - FDA Notices of Judgment Collection, 1908-1966." Nih.gov, June 1945.

American Institute of Architects. "Merit Award: Residence." Architects' Report, vol. 6, no. 1, 1963.

Auld, Frank D. "Fred Douglass as a Slave in the Auld Family." The Evening Sun, 20 Aug. 1925.

Baltimore Heritage. "Meadow Mill." Explore Baltimore Heritage.

Beirne, Francis F. The Amiable Baltimoreans. JHU Press, 1984.

Bishop, Audrey. "By Any Name as Sweet." The Baltimore Sun, 16 Nov. 1958.

Brennessel, Barbara. Diamonds in the Marsh. Waltham, MA, Brandeis University Press, 2021.

"Bryden B. Hyde Obituary." The Star-Democrat, 3 Jan. 2002.

CHM Staff. ""Meals by Fred Harvey" - Chicago History Museum." Chicago History Museum, 11 Feb. 2021.

Dilts, James D. "He Sings at Breakfast." The Sun, 26 Nov. 1967.

Dorsey, John. "Mount Vernon Place." The Baltimore Sun, 7 June 1970.

Eugster, David, and Translated from German by Cathy Hickley. The Chocolate Treat at the Heart of a Swiss Racism Debate. 16 June 2020.

"Feast for Eyes and Palate." The Baltimore Sun, 23 Nov. 1910.

Foods of the world. Recipes : The Cooking of Vienna's Empire. Alexandria, VA, Time-Life Books, 1974.

"Four Cases Instituted —Mr. C. Harry Friend Gets Divorce." The Balltimore Sun, 8 Apr. 1901.

"George Ray Hyde Funeral Friday." The Evening Sun, 6 Mar. 1952.

"H. J. McGrath Dies at Seaside." The Baltimore Sun, 25 Feb. 1909.

"Hackerman House - Former Thomas-Jencks-Gladding House Now Part of the Walters Art Museum | Explore Baltimore Heritage." Explore Baltimore Heritage, 2025.

Hood College. "The Harold Weisberg Archive." Hood.edu.

"Indianerkrapfen." Blogspot.com, 2025. Accessed 14 Sept. 2025.

"J WM Junkins Catsup Baltimore MD Maryland Antique Fancy Shape Ketchup Bottle." Worthpoint, 2018. Accessed 28 Sept. 2025.

Janvier, Meredith. Baltimore Yesterdays. Baltimore, MD, H.G. Roebuck & Son, 1937.

Kinzer, Stephen. The Brothers: John Foster Dulles, Allen Dulles, and Their Secret World War. Macmillan, 2013.

Komlos, John. Louis Kossuth in America, 1851-1852. East European Institute, 1973.

Lally, Kathy. "Hydes Took Mansion with Them, in Pieces." The Baltimore Sun, 30 Oct. 1977.

"Marker of the Fredericksburg (Virginia) Artillery at Gettysburg." The Battle of Gettysburg.

McGrain, John. "Purveyors of Baltimore History: William B. Marye (1886-1979)." Rememberingbaltimore.net, 3 Nov. 2019.

"Mr. A. D. Clemens Dead." The Baltimore Sun, 11 Nov. 1909.

"Mrs. Preston Says Husband "Is Most Wonderful Man."" The Evening Sun, 6 Mar. 1923.

Northern Arizona University. "Menus, Fred Harvey Company." Nau.edu.

Novak, Josephine. "Mrs. McKeldin Sees an Easier Pace for Pat Hughes." The Evening Sun, 5 Dec. 1978.

Pietila, Antero. Not in My Neighborhood. Ivan R. Dee Publisher, 2010.

"Prize Recipe Contest No. 1." The San Francisco Examiner, 5 Jan. 1901.

Shalhope, Robert E. The Baltimore Bank Riot. University of Illinois Press, 2009.

Srodes, James. Allen Dulles Master of Spies. Regnery Publishing, 2000.

Talbot, David. The Devil's Chessboard Allen Dulles, the CIA, and the Rise of America's Secret Government. New York, Harper Perennial, 2016.

"The Canned Goods Trade 1909-02-26: Vol 31 Iss 27." Internet Archive, 1909.

United States. Food and Drug Administration. Notices of Judgment Under the Food And Drugs Act. Washington: Govt. print. off.,1908.

Walters Art Museum. Autograph Letter from Sybby Grant to Her Enslaver, John Hanson Thomas.

Weaver, Diane E. Maryland Women and the Transformation of Politics, 1890s-1930, University of Maryland, College Park, United States -- Maryland, 1992.

White, Joyce. "Kossuth Cakes: A Maryland Culinary Relic." A Taste of History with Joyce White, 2014.

Wikipedia. "Baltimore Bank Riot." Wikipedia.org, Wikimedia Foundation, Inc.

Wikipedia. "American Politician and Mayor of Baltimore 1911-1919." Wikipedia.org, Wikimedia Foundation, Inc.

William, Stump. "Man in the Street: Louis Kossuth." The Baltimore Sun, 25 June 1950.

Woman's College of Baltimore. The Woman's College of Baltimore.[Baltimore, Md.: Woman's College of Baltimore,1898.

Woman's Educational Industrial Union of Auburn, New York. The Woman's Union Cook Book. [The Women's Educational and Industrial Union], 1932.

Woman Suffrage of Maryland Collection, Special Collections, Enoch Pratt Free Library/Maryland's State Library Resource Center.

Robert acted as a messenger during the campaigns and was many times the confidante of political secrets known to but few. Robert accompanied his master on all of his out-of-town trips and always administered to his personal wants.

spect of the members for their deceased friend was passed and will be sent to the family. Mr. Louis P. Hennighausen, the president, is ill at his home, but sent a letter expressing regret that he could not attend the meeting.

GENERAL LATROBE'S FAVORITE POEM OF THE "OLD GRAY MARE" SERIES

"THE OLD GRAY MARE'S ADDRESS TO THE PEOPLE OF THE BELT."
[Composed by Edward O'Mahony and sung by Thomas F. McNulty.]

My name is Lizzie, the "old gray mare."
  Whose deeds are famed in song:
On the subject of annexation
  My opinion is very strong.
It is not a political measure,
  No party issue is felt—
The question is simply to decide:
  "Shall Baltimore have the 'Belt'?"
    [Chorus.]

From Highlandtown to Garrison lane
  Upon this mission stumping,
In sleet and snow, hail and rain,
  "Ferdy" keeps me jumping.
For old Lizzle's sake, give him his way.
  'Twill save me many a welt
If you, good folks, will only say
  You'll let him have the "Belt."
    [Chorus.]

His name is Latrobe, as you well know:
  Of Baltimore he is Mayor.
He comes among your people to show
  The advantages you'll share
By annexation with us,
  That fact will soon be felt
In protection to life and property
  Of citizens of the "Belt."
    [Chorus.]

He'll grade and pave and curb your
    streets,
  Give you water and public schools,
With a gallant fire department
  And police to enforce the rules
That make a quiet community;
  Their power will soon be felt
In wiping out the thugs and thieves
  That terrorize the "Belt."
    [Chorus.]

Your taxes, rates and costs are made
  As low as you can ask.
On your patriotism we rely
  To aid us in this task.
"Bone of our bone," "flesh of our flesh,"
  Have we not fairly dealt?
I ask you could we offer more
  To the residents of the "Belt?"
    [Chorus.]

We are Baltimoreans, all of us.
  Wherever we reside,
Out in the "Belt" or in the town,
  In Baltimore we take pride.
With a hundred thousand people more
  Our progress will be felt;
A higher rank 'mong cities we'll take
  When we annex the "Belt."
    [Chorus.]

Fair Baltimore, with blushing cheek,
  Within your lusty arms
Lies hugged and girdled round about,
  While you gaze on her charms.
She asks that you complete the match
  And let yourself be felt:
In such a case it isn't right
  To only be a "Belt."
    [Chorus.]

And therefore to the ladies
  "Old Liz" makes this appeal:
Go make your husbands, and sweethearts
    too,
  This happy union seal
By voting for annexation.
  Then this boundary line will melt.
You'll all be "Baltimore beauties" then,
  Not "ladies of the 'Belt.'"
    [Chorus.]

Another "Liz" ballad, written by Mr. O'Mahony, was sung by Mr. McNulty in the campaign of 1887. The first and last stanzas are as follows:

My name is Latrobe, as you well know,
  I'm a candidate for Mayor,
And if I only get a show,
  You may bet I will get there.
I am on the go from morn till night,
  In rain or in sunshine;
Myself and Lizzie—that's the name
  Of that old gray mare of mine.

I "spec" that when the old mare dies
  She'll join some angel band;
With silver shoes upon her feet,
  She'll prance the golden strand;
And when Reformers gather 'round
  She'll lift her heels behind
And kick them into kingdom come,
  That old gray mare of mine.